# A HEART

## AFTER GOD

# Books by Elizabeth Hoekstra

*Be Still*

*A Heart After God*

# A HEART
## AFTER GOD

—

## ELIZABETH M. HOEKSTRA

BETHANY HOUSE PUBLISHERS
*Minneapolis, Minnesota*

Published by Bethany House Publishers
A Ministry of Bethany Fellowship International
11400 Hampshire Avenue South
Bloomington, Minnesota 55438
www.bethanyhouse.com

Printed in the United States of America by
Bethany Press International, Bloomington, Minnesota 55438

Library of Congress Cataloging-in-Publication Data

Hoekstra, Elizabeth M., 1962–
    A Heart after God : loving him with heart, soul, mind, and strength /
by Elizabeth M. Hoekstra.
        p.   cm.
    ISBN 0-7642-2548-0 (pbk.)
    1.  Christian life.   I.  Title.
    BV4501.3 .H+      2002
248.8′43—dc21                                              2001005672

*To Peter, my best friend*

*I can't imagine walking this journey*

*to the heart of our shared Lord without you.*

ELIZABETH M. HOEKSTRA founded Direct Path Ministries in 1997, a writing and speaking ministry that encourages and equips her readers and listeners to "walk in the Word." This is her tenth book. She and her family make their home in New Hampshire.

# ACKNOWLEDGMENTS

The words "it's iron sharpening iron" are not necessarily what a writer wants to hear from an editor upon rejection of a manuscript. But thanks to my more-than-an-editor, Steve Laube, senior editor of nonfiction at Bethany House, his challenge sparked my ire and made me sharpen my pencil for another attempt. Steve, thank you for asking the right questions, giving me the impetus for this book.

A humble nod to Louise Greene, whose honesty and writing integrity I admire and to which I aspire. Louise, thanks for meeting my need for help in the eleventh hour.

To my family: Peter, Geneva, and Jordan, who not only unselfishly but also *willingly* pay the price for the cost of my career. Family, thanks for modeling humility.

And to my mom, Cindy D. Marriner, my faithful cheerleader.

# CONTENTS

*Hear, O Israel:*

*The Lord our God, the Lord is one.*

*Love the Lord your God with all your heart*

*and with all your soul*

*and with all your strength.*

*These commandments that I give you today*

*are to be upon your hearts.*

DEUTERONOMY 6:4–6

# Introduction

---

A couple of years ago an interviewer for a magazine asked me who I most identify with in the Bible. The question held my imagination for a time. I could have nodded to any number of biblical women: I'm as bull-headed stubborn as Deborah. I skip between Mary and Martha in busyness and devotion at my Savior's feet. I'm courageous in crisis like Esther, and I strive to be the Proverbs 31 "wife of noble character." Despite all that, I had to answer that I see myself the most in King David.

David's life isn't just a revealing slice of humanity, it's the whole pie. His life as shepherd, poet, warrior, adulterer, murderer, and king draws a vivid picture of all our crimson-colored depravity. Yet David may well be known most as the "man after God's heart." He didn't have the advantage of a personal relationship with Christ as we do. David still had to offer animal sacrifices for his sins. And the blood flowed pretty thick at times for him! He knew God loved him and forgave him for his misdeeds, but because his Redeemer hadn't walked the earth yet, King David didn't experience the saving grace you and I know from God's sacrificing His one and only Son.

In the twenty-first century our hearts may rest in the grace-land of Calvary, but our actions speak of living on the San Andreas fault line. We act as though it's a split-life decision between Christ and our sinful nature. Jesus himself said, "If a house is divided against itself, that house cannot stand" (Mark 3:25).

King David lived perpetually on the edge of this gaping fault line. He trembled at the thought of how deep into trouble his heart could take him. That's why he cried to the Lord, "Give me an undivided heart, that I may fear your name" (Psalm 86:11).

And that's where I most identify with David. His split heart feels familiar to me; yet I too desire to be a woman after God's heart with an undivided heart for Him alone. Psalm 86:11 has long held me hostage. The words *undivided heart* won't let me go. Like a short tether, these words keep pulling my will back to who is at the center of my heart and life: the Lord, or me?

By nature I'm an all-or-nothing person. I figure if I'm going to own one pet, I might as well care for twelve. If I'm going to vacuum the living room, I might as well vacuum the whole house. If I'm going to plan a hike, I might as well set my feet to the entire Appalachian Trail.

This same determined, wholehearted commitment is what led me to ask, "Who is this Lord that I want to know by name and character and to love with an unwavering heart?" It felt like a puzzle that I needed to piece together.

What do we know about Him? First and foremost, He knows you and me by name. He knows every part of our being—inside and out. He knows we're sinful. He knows we fail. We aren't a mystery to Him.

Yet a sense of mystery traces the relationship we have with Him, doesn't it? The intrigue lies in *our desire to know His heart*. We want to know Him, to understand Him, to grasp His character, and to live in His wisdom.

The mystery of these things is our inheritance as children in His family. The treasury of God's heart for you and me is overflowing. He *wants* us to experience His character. He *wants* us to seek His heart: to know it, understand it, and act on what we learn. Why would He want us to solve these mysteries about Him? Because He loves us.

Paul referred to the mystery of God's love for us through the coming of Christ when he wrote, "The mystery that has been kept hidden for ages and generations, but is now disclosed to the saints. To them God has chosen to make known among the Gentiles the glorious riches of this mystery, which is Christ in you, the hope of glory" (Colossians 1:26–27). "Christ in you"? Christ at the center of our whole hearts.

Christ is the final clue to the mystery of God's heart. His words and actions and faith are the answers to seeking and finding God's heart. The entire Bible, the *Word* from God's mouth, tells us who He is and for whom His heart yearns. It yearns for you and me. Ephesians 3:17–19 confirms this: "so that Christ may dwell in your hearts through faith. And I pray that you, being rooted and established in love, may have power, together with all the saints, to grasp how wide and long and high and deep is the love of Christ, and to know this love that surpasses knowledge—that you may be filled to the measure of all the fullness of God."

What a love! Furthermore, nothing, absolutely *nothing* can bar God's love from us. Like Paul, I too am convinced "that neither death nor life, neither angels nor demons, neither the present nor the future, nor any powers, neither height nor depth, nor anything else in all creation, will be able to separate us from the love of God that is in Christ Jesus our Lord" (Romans 8:38–39).

There is no doubt that God loves us; Christ loves us. It's unearned. It's unstoppable. There is only one thing the Lord asks: that we adore and love Him with all of our hearts as He is at the center of our lives. He wants our undivided love in return.

When Jesus spoke of the greatest commandment in Mark 12:29–30, He was answering a veiled question about the mystery of knowing God's heart and for whom our heart should beat: "'The most important one,' answered Jesus, 'is this: "Hear, O Israel, the Lord our God, the Lord is one. Love the Lord your God with all your heart and with all your soul and with all your mind and with all your strength."'"

Why did Jesus say this is the greatest commandment? *Because that's how God loves us*: He loves all of our being, with all of His heart. Why does He demand our full-strength love in return? *Because anything else is less than enough*. "For the Lord, whose name is Jealous, is a jealous God" (Exodus 34:14). He jealously guards His relationship with us so nothing else tip-toes onto the center stage of our hearts.

*A Heart After God* is about wholeheartedly welcoming the Lord at the center of your heart by loving Him with all of your heart, soul, mind, and strength.

Look at it this way: imagine a beautiful picture frame. Each side of the frame represents the straight edge of one of these four areas of our lives: heart, soul, mind, and strength. What are they framing? What's at the center of these defining lines of our lives? Our Lord Jesus Christ should be. Our heart-love, soul-love, mind-love, and strength-love hem Jesus in at the center.

This concept is important to grasp. Another way to un-derstand it is to ask yourself, "Who is 'on center' in my heart?" Or, "Who has the central place in my thoughts and actions?"

We may know this is the picture that we want to adorn the walls of our lives, but how? Where can we turn to learn *how* to love the Lord with *more* of our heart, soul, mind, and strength? To where God meets the man-need of humanity: Scripture.

*A Heart After God* takes examples of people from Scripture and shows how the godly characters expressed love for the Lord with their heart, soul, mind, and strength. The Lord was at the center of their lives. We have much to learn from their models. These were sinful people—like you and me. They were men and women who desired to love God more, to do the right thing, and to be faithful—regardless of their circum-stances. These men and women loved God in war and in peace. They loved Him in fear and in happiness. They loved Him at home and in their communities. They loved Him in persecution and in joy. They loved Him in loss and death and hope and perseverance.

But even more enduring is that through each encounter with the Lord they experienced His character. Though our twenty-first-century culture differs from that of the Old and New Testaments, parallels exist simply because of the ongoing nature of humanity. Walk their journeys with me and learn about the Lord's character while loving Him into the center of your life with all of your heart, soul, mind, and strength.

# How to Use This Book

---

This book has forty meditations in ten chapters. Each chapter is divided into four readings—heart, soul, mind, and strength—where we'll study how the biblical characters demonstrated whole-hearted love for the Lord, placing Him at the center of their lives.

Each chapter begins with Scripture. Allow the words of our Lord to captivate your heart. You are facing a challenging lifestyle choice of who is *on center* in your heart.

At the conclusion of each day's reading is a prayer for drawing closer to the Lord. Some people like written prayers, others don't. The point isn't that you pray the exact words, but that you spend time meditating about what the Lord would have you learn to draw closer to His heart.

Similarly, each chapter concludes with a revelation about God's character, a prayer challenge of "who is 'on center' in your life?" and a memory verse. If you struggle with memorizing Scripture, try thinking of it this way: The Bible reveals who the Lord is, how He acts, and what His heart and mind are. Just as you memorize the faces and features of those you love, so too can you memorize the "face" and character features of God—through His Holy Word.

Last, but most important, as the Lord takes His rightful place at the center of your heart, please pray earnestly. Pray for a heart willing to be broken and mended by His hand, a soul thirsting to drink deeply from His Word, a mind ripe to absorb His wisdom, and a body fit to use for His glory.

# I

# A PICTURE OF LOVE:

## *Loving Him With Everything*

TO KNOW HIM AS

## *LOVER of the SOUL*

READ: DEUTERONOMY 5–8

# HEART

*These commandments that I give you today*
*are to be upon your hearts.*

DEUTERONOMY 6:6

When I was six years old, my parents went on a canoeing trip, leaving my sisters and me with a baby-sitter. My father had just bought us a new bicycle, and it was my turn to use it, even though I was too small for the frame and still pretty wobbly without training wheels. Sure enough, I fell off on the gravelly edge of the road. I sat in the dirt and brushed off my knees. My hands came away sticky, and I looked with fascination at my right knee as blood oozed around a half-inch-diameter rock embedded in my flesh. Even as this thought jelled in my brain, pain knuckled my leg, and I realized I had *a rock in my knee!*

The sitter called a family friend, telling her of my accident. This friend happened to be a nurse, and she took me to the doctor who, with what felt like too little anesthesia, removed the rock. Six stitches and thirty-some years later, I live with a scar in my right knee.

I remember the pain of that incident, but even more, I remember how once the rock and the grit were cleaned out and the area washed, it felt good. Yes, it ached some, but nothing like the pain of something in the flesh that shouldn't be there.

We all have debris in our lives that causes us pain. And no place is this more evident than in our heart. It's a place invisible to man, but fully knowable to God. Like a skilled and gentle surgeon, the Lord wants to perform surgery on our heart. Why is surgery needed? To remove the debris—the stuff that gets in the way of His filling our heart. Our heart needs to be fully in His hands so it can more fully hear Him, know Him, and be like Him.

In the decree of loving the Lord with *all* of our heart, soul, mind, and strength, God started from the inside, because all of our actions are motivated by what's in our heart. "As water reflects a face, so a man's heart reflects the man" (Proverbs 27:19).

Naturally Jesus understood this concept. He was in the process of answering the Pharisees' questions about delivering a demon-possessed man, and how evil and godliness cannot coexist, when He spoke these words: "For out of the overflow of the heart the mouth speaks. The good man brings good things out of the good stored up in him, and the evil man brings evil things out of the evil stored up in him" (Matthew 12:34–35). *Stored up?*

What's overflowing in the bin of our heart? Is it love, or . . . anger, pride, deceit, unforgiveness, fear? Why could that list go on and on? Because there's so much debris overflowing into our hearts!

But the command says to love the Lord God with *all* our heart. If we're loving Him with all our heart, there won't be any room left for other issues. This seems like an impossibility, doesn't it? Of course it is. Sin separates us from a heart perfectly full of love. Because we live in a sin-filled world, where sin is always edging our heart, love for God has to constantly elbow its way to stay at center stage in our heart.

*Because we live in a sin-filled world, where sin is always edging our heart, love for God has to constantly elbow its way to stay at center stage in our heart.*

King Solomon understood this struggle to maintain center-stage love. After the temple of the Lord was completed, he offered a beautiful, lengthy, praise-filled prayer of dedication to the Lord. Solomon ended the prayer with this charge to the nation: "But your hearts must be *fully committed* to the Lord our God, to live by his decrees and obey his commands, *as at this time*" (1 Kings 8:61, italics added).

He reminded them that it was easy to feel overwhelming love for God right then. Debris in their hearts was at an all-time low. This was most definitely the highlight of their lives: the completion and dedication of the temple of the Lord. Solomon challenged them to stay committed to God even when the emotional high passed.

That's what loving God with all of our heart means for us in the twenty-first century. We need to stay committed to loving Him even when we're tired, even when it hurts, even when it doesn't make sense, even when debris and grit need to be removed from our hearts. It's a commitment *of* love *to* love God above all else.

"For the eyes of the Lord range throughout the earth to strengthen those whose hearts are fully committed to him" (2 Chronicles 16:9).

## DRAWING CLOSER TODAY

*Lord, I'll trust you to grow a deeper commitment in my heart to love you with more of my heart. Thank you for your faithfulness and absolute love for me.*

# SOUL

*Love the Lord your God . . . with all
your soul.*

DEUTERONOMY 6:5

A number of years ago I attended a benefit concert. This type of event is no doubt familiar: a performing artist donates her time and talent, people who attend pay a fee or give a free-will offering, then the funds generated from the event go to support a ministry, cause, or organization. I attended the concert, and the funds donated were to help support the local pregnancy center—a ministry to which I felt a deep attachment.

This concept of "benefit" is key to our faith-walk with the Lord. Christ's death profits our soul. Without His offering as a living sacrifice, our soul would not hold a secure place in heaven.

I love the definition of *benefit* in my dictionary: "Anything contributing to an improvement of condition." Christ's death certainly contributes to the improvement of the human condition. Think where our souls would end up if not for His "contribution." Heaven cannot be compared to hell.

King David understood this full well when he wrote, "Praise the Lord, O my soul; all my inmost being, praise his holy name. Praise the Lord, O my soul, and forget not all his *benefits*—who forgives all your sins" (Psalm 103:1–3, italics added).

It is for our soul's profit to love the Lord with all our heart, soul, mind, and strength. How do we show the love in our soul for the Lord? When we accept Christ's death and resurrection as the *benefit* our soul needs for eternal life.

*It is for our soul's profit to love the Lord with all our heart, soul, mind, and strength.*

What is the point of this blessed gain? An answer is found in Matthew 12:22, which tells of one of the many times Jesus healed an ailment and cast out demons in a suffering person. "Then they brought him a demon-possessed man who was blind and mute, and Jesus healed him, so that he could both talk and see." This story may be short on words, but it's long on implication. From this brief encounter, Jesus preaches about the diametric opposition of good and evil. He says, "But if I drive out demons by the Spirit of God, then the kingdom of God has come upon you" (12:28). What does this tell us? When Christ healed this demon-possessed man (and every other possessed person He healed), it was the man's *soul* Jesus was interested in. The healing of his ears and eyes were an added gain, but the man's soul is what was of utmost importance to Christ.

In Luke, a different man healed from evil possession was instructed by Jesus to go and tell everyone what had happened (Luke 8:26–39). "Return home and tell how much God has done for you" (v. 39). So the man went away and told all over town how much Jesus had done for him. He probably had to say very little—he had been in chains, so strong was the possession. His healing spoke louder than words: his soul-love for the Lord likely showed in his from-then-on daily confession of what Jesus had done for him.

Does our soul speak louder than our words? We can live in a complete soul-love circle: Christ's death profits our soul and our soul-love for Him benefits those who are witnesses to Christ in our life.

Christ is all for our soul. Our soul needs to be all for Christ. Will you accept the advantage for your soul and then benefit God's glory with your witness of who He is?

## DRAWING CLOSER TODAY

*Lord, I thank you for the benefit you have guaranteed to my soul through your death and resurrection. I desire to benefit your kingdom with my full soul-love. I pray for boldness as you put opportunities in my path to tell how much you have done for me.*

# MIND

*Hear, O Israel: The Lord our God, the*
*Lord is one.*

DEUTERONOMY 6:4

I n Mark's account of the greatest commandment, why did Jesus begin His answer with the *full* quote from Deuteronomy? (Mark 12:29). Why not cut right to the meat, right to the heart, if you will, of the command? Why not just say *what* we are to do as God-following Christians?

Because first He had to say *who* this command came from and *why* the command was necessary. Our mind needs to understand this before our heart and soul can act on it.

The Lord's salutation gives us the answers we're looking for.

I. *Hear*: First, before we can love God with our entire being, we have to be listening. How can we possibly love something if we aren't paying attention, listening, or hearing?

We need to learn to identify God's voice. *Did I hear Him whisper in the breeze during my morning walk?* Our heart needs to be tuned to our God-frequency, and constantly retuned to eliminate competing static. At the center of every person's heart are the words *ear* and *hear*.

*At the center of every person's heart are the words ear and hear.*

2. *O Israel*: Who is this command for? His chosen people. It's interesting where this command occurs in the Bible: sandwiched after the meat of the Ten Commandments and before the Israelites entered the Promised Land, flowing with milk and honey. In this place of physical uncertainty, the Lord assured them of their place in His heart. Deuteronomy 7:6 says, "For you are a people holy to the Lord your God. The Lord has chosen you out of all the peoples on the face of the earth to be his people, his treasured possession." That's not just for the Israelites delivered from Egypt. We, too, are His treasured possession. Paul says in Romans 8:17 that we are "heirs of God and co-heirs with Christ."

Before God could deliver the Israelites to this rich land He had promised them, they needed to understand their relationship to Him and what He expected of them. He was leading them into a clearly defined territory, with equally clearly defined laws of God.

The Ten Commandments are relationship guidelines: our relationship to God and to others around us. That is why it makes so much sense that this "greatest commandment" is

centered between the Ten Commandments and the Promised
Land. That's why this "greatest commandment" is so *great*:
When we love God with those four areas of our being, the
Ten Commandments become the framework for living a
godly life.

3. *The Lord our God*: Whose God? *Our* God. This speaks of
unity under the Lord. It speaks of our relationship with God
and our relationship with one another. Though we have an
up-close-and-personal relationship with the Lord through
Jesus Christ, we are also united with each other. Paul says in
Romans 12:5, "So in Christ we who are many form one body,
and each member belongs to all the others." As Christians, we
may act independently, but the ripples touch everyone, good
or bad.

In the context of the greatest commandment, when we
love the Lord with our entire being, the unity of the church
can't help but be affected, because an individual, personal motivation of love for God brings the second command—loving
our neighbors—to pass. This is the unity implied by the words
*our God.*

4. *The Lord is one*: Who are we to love so entirely? The one
and only God. The God of the universe. The Creator, the
Author and Perfecter of our lives and our faith. Our Abba
Father. The Alpha and the Omega. He may have different
names, but He is one.

Our lifelong pursuit is to know the one and only God.
Who this God is that we serve was not only the Israelites'
birthright but also our reason for being and our hope for the
future.

## DRAWING CLOSER TODAY

*Lord God, thank you that you are my God and the same God of all my Christian brothers and sisters. Help me to stay single-minded and focused on you as my one and only Lord.*

# STRENGTH

*Love the Lord your God ... with all
your strength.*

DEUTERONOMY 6:5

One of my son's favorite pastimes is arm wrestling. Two-handed, he can beat me. When he's locked in a battle, his little arm shakes, his face turns red, his eyebrows furrow, and his body tenses. With his whole body and strength he's trying to win the arm lock, pushing against my hand with everything he's got.

This is the image I have when I think about loving God with all of my strength. Every muscle fiber bound for the task. Body alert and ready to issue extreme effort and concentration on my desire to love God with all of me.

The problem, of course, is that we can't embrace God and give Him a bear hug to show our full-strength love. We have to show it in a different way. But how?

This dilemma brings to mind the rich young ruler in Luke 18:18–30. He found himself in a predicament. When he asked Jesus how he could inherit eternal life, Jesus answered by reminding him of five of the Ten Commandments. They were the "honesty" commandments—the "don't commit adultery, murder, steal, or lie, and be sure to keep your family name good." The rich ruler enthusiastically said he had kept all of them, probably certain that Jesus would say, "You're in!"

But Jesus knew his heart and what resided there. He said, "You still lack one thing. Sell everything you have and give to the poor, and you will have treasure in heaven. Then come, follow me" (v. 22).

What was He saying? "Yes, your beliefs have motivated you to act wisely, but in your heart *are you loving God with all you've got?*" This is where the conviction of loving God internally transitions to external action. The rich ruler had obeyed the commands, but had he obeyed them because he loved God above all else? If he had obeyed the commands out of love for God, then selling everything would not have been too much to ask.

What's the end of the story about the rich young ruler? He went away sad. It would have taken determined perseverance for him to sell everything. He just couldn't do it. The strength of his love for God wasn't enough for him to take the necessary steps to be able to follow Christ wholeheartedly.

This is the reason why Christ included *strength* in His answer to the greatest command question as compared to Deuteronomy, which includes only heart, soul, and mind. Because the actions of our lives need to be purposed for God's plan.

Our strength-love for the Lord can't be constructed by any other means.

Loving the Lord with all our strength is how we put undivided love into action. Jesus asked the rich ruler to sell everything. What "everything" is He asking us to "sell"? For some of us it may be our personal treasures that maneuver into the center of our lives, creating a wall between God and us. For others, it may mean leaving behind attitudes or actions that rob us of our strength.

*The actions of our lives need to be purposed for God's plan.*

Loving God with all our strength is an act of perseverance. "Let us throw off everything that hinders and the sin that so easily entangles, and let us run with perseverance the race marked out for us. Let us fix our eyes on Jesus, the author and perfecter of our faith, who for the joy set before him endured the cross, scorning its shame, and sat down at the right hand of the throne of God. *Consider him who endured such opposition from sinful men, so that you will not grow weary and lose heart*" (Hebrews 12:1–3, italics added). When our strength-love for God wanes, these verses remind us that Christ persevered through pain and death, and how His endurance can renew our strength. Our inspiration for full-strength love comes from Christ's strength on the cross.

DRAWING CLOSER TODAY

*Lord, on my own I cannot have enough strength to love you with all of me. But I know I can love you with the strength that is mine through Christ. Thank you for that assurance.*

TO KNOW HIM AS

# LOVER of the SOUL

Understanding the "whys" and "what fors" of the greatest commandment leaves no doubt as to the Father God's love for us. He is the Lover of our souls. He knows us intimately, and He loves us down to the depths of who we are. First John 4:12 tells us that because God lives in us His love is made complete in us. With full-strength love for Him in our heart, His heart and ours are joined together as one—just as married lovers are complete in the unity of one flesh, we become one flesh with God's heart.

*Who is "on center" in your life?*

Will you commit to persevere in single-minded devotion as you follow after the Lord's heart?

Memory Verse:
*Teach me your way, O Lord, and I will walk in your truth; give me an undivided heart, that I may fear your name.*

PSALM 86:11

# 2

# A MOTHER'S HEART:

*Loving Him When Life Doesn't Make Sense*

TO KNOW HIM AS

## WONDERFUL COUNSELOR

READ: LUKE 2:21–52

# HEART

*But his mother treasured all these things in
her heart.*

We can take nothing at only face value in the Bible. There are layers upon layers, and parallels running side-by-side, linking the Old Testament to the New Testament and connecting both with us. God's Word is for every person—it's not a that-was-then-and-this-is-now study—because the commonality of life means that the Word of God has personal life application for yesterday, today, and tomorrow.

Just as the Trinity of God the Father, Son, and Holy Spirit is threefold, so is His Word three-dimensional: first, it's the language He uses to talk to us; second, are the actual events and characters in the Bible; and third, is the take-away value for us personally—the meaning behind the meaning. We can be sure that nothing is only an inch deep and a mile wide with the Lord and His Word.

An example of the third dimension is found in Mary, the mother of Jesus. We can learn a lot from her about how to love all of God with all our heart. She certainly had a heart after God. She knew she had been chosen for a miracle, and she willingly and humbly accepted the job God had entrusted to her: raise His Son, born from her flesh.

At the conclusion of the previous chapter, we saw how the Lord is the Lover of our souls, and how when we love Him heart, soul, mind, and strength, we become "one flesh" with Him. Mary had "one flesh" with God the Father. She was one in heart with Him. When the Spirit of the Lord came upon her and impregnated her with Jesus, she was one in soul with Him. Then she gave birth to the Christ—His squalling little body came from her flesh, born in pain, like any other child born of a woman. From her flesh came Christ, in the flesh. This is a layer below a layer: only Christ in the flesh, born from the flesh of a woman, could save us, through His man-death, from the manifestation of our flesh—sin.

Mary wasn't privy to the end of the story, though. We have the advantage of knowing the end from the beginning. She didn't, so each revelation was met with wonder about just who this little boy was that she and Joseph were raising. Look at the words used to describe Joseph's and her feelings: "marveled," "amazed," "astonished," "anxiously searching," and "did not understand" (Luke 2:33, 47–48, 50). Remarkably, although these feelings cast thoughts of confusion on what and who Jesus was, Mary is said to have "treasured all these things in her heart."

There's a silence implied with the word *treasured*. We don't hear much more from Mary after this point in Scripture. She's silent. Maybe she simply continued to feel marvel at who this man was that she had borne.

*Each revelation was met with wonder about just who this little boy was that she and Joseph were raising.*

In the silent treasury of her heart, she was trusting God, the same God with whom she had a heart-love relationship. She only had half of the information about her son during His growing-up years. Though she had been warned that a sword would pierce her soul (2:35), she couldn't have anticipated the pure anguish that would beset her at the injustice of her son's death. She couldn't foretell the future. Neither can we—in raising our children or in anything.

It's said that hindsight is twenty/twenty vision. It's "Aha! Now I get it!" Life with the Lord is like a Polaroid picture: the developing picture has blurry edges until the process is complete. How often does the Lord give us only half the picture? I'd venture to say pretty frequently. Sometimes we have to wait for full understanding of the third dimension of His Word. Why? Because we need to treasure in our heart those things that we *do know*, and trust Him for the rest.

What do we know that we can hold dear in our heart? That God loves us, He is in control, and He does know the whole picture. Paul says it this way: "Now we see but a poor reflection as in a mirror; then we shall see face to face. Now

I know in part; then I shall know fully, even as I am fully known" (1 Corinthians 13:12).

DRAWING CLOSER TODAY
*Lord, thank you that you do know fully, while I only know in part. I pray that I will be able to treasure the truths I know about you and then leave the rest up to you.*

# SOUL

*Then Simeon blessed them and said to Mary, his mother: "This child is destined to cause the falling and rising of many in Israel, and to be a sign that will be spoken against, so that the thoughts of many hearts will be revealed. And a sword will pierce your own soul too."*

LUKE 2:34–35

Disappointment distances us from our hopes, dreams, and desires. It seems as though the hopes are like a faint light across an expanse of unnavigable stormy seas. The prefix "dis" means "away" or "apart from." That's what *dis*appointment means: we are apart from an "appointment"—something that we wanted to happen.

As parents we will inevitably feel disappointment about our children. That's not easy to admit, because we expect from the first moment we cradle them in our arms that we'll forever love them with the same level of adoration. But they carry their own slice of humanity, and inevitably they'll disappoint us. Maybe they don't follow the career we hoped for them, maybe they choose a lifestyle we know is sin. Or maybe something happens to them over which we have no control, and it imprints them, and us, with hurt.

On the heels of disappointment is confusion. We may stand before the Lord, stuttering, "But . . . but . . . but . . ." We don't understand, and we'd like some sort of explanation.

Christ's mother, like us, would experience a period of spiritual confusion. Simeon prophesied that Mary's soul would be pierced. She would suffer not only a broken heart, but her very faith would be pierced and challenged. Figuratively speaking, her soul was pierced when a sword pierced Christ's side as He hung on the cross. He had been born of her flesh and heart and soul. The soldiers might as well have thrust a sword through Mary too.

Imagine the injustice she must have felt at this betrayal of *her son*. If your child has ever been wrongly accused of anything, you know how hot indignation burned in your soul. Even more, that fire would be justifiable if your child was violated in any way. How out of control Mary must have felt!

Her soul was pierced. Her soul was split. Her soul must have felt divided between love for her son and love for God. She loved her son as a mother loves her child—born of her flesh. But how could the God she'd trusted and loved for so long take her son, *His Son*, in this way!?

Our soul feels pierced too when it seems as though something God has entrusted to us is ripped from our heart. It's *dis*appointment again. What we thought the Lord had "appointed" to us—a dream, a hope, a plan—feels painfully distant. When this happens, it seems that trust is broken with our Lord, because we know He knows the desire of our heart, and He knows one of those desires is that we'd rather not feel any pain.

> *When we have a soul pierced with pain it shakes our beliefs to the very core of our relationship with God.*

When we have a soul pierced with pain it shakes our beliefs to the very core of our relationship with God. A picture comes to mind of a pear tree being violently shaken. The hard-won ripe fruit smashes to the ground—bruising, breaking open, with bits scattering everywhere. It's somewhat how we feel, isn't it? Separated from our Lord and in pieces emotionally. We may well say, "But that was *good fruit* (a good hope, a good plan, a good dream) in me that was just discarded!" Mary may also have been thinking as she looked on at the foot of the cross, *But He's so good. He's just beginning to help people see God. This can't be the end!*

But maybe the "fruit" isn't the point when we've been shaken and soul-pierced. Maybe the relationship with the "tree" is the larger issue. In our soul-love relationship with the Lord, sometimes we have to return to the basics, especially when we're pierced through by pain. What are the basics? God loved us first, and He'll love us to the last. He's an always and forever God. The point is, will we trust Him even when we feel pierced through? Are we willing to wait it out to see how He will be glorified, despite our confusion, disappointment, and pain?

DRAWING CLOSER TODAY

*Lord, I thank you for being my God always and forever. I thank you that Christ's death on the wooden cross was the "tree of life" for me. I pray that when my soul feels pierced, I'll remember the point of the pain: I'm learning to trust you, and I know you will be glorified.*

# MIND

*Everyone who heard him was amazed at his understanding and his answers. When his parents saw him, they were astonished. His mother said to him, "Son, why have you treated us like this? Your father and I have been anxiously searching for you."*

*"Why were you searching for me?" he asked. "Didn't you know I had to be in my Father's house?"*

LUKE 2:47–49

When I was a child, my family lived on a farm of open fields and acres of woodland. We didn't have any neighbors nearby, so my sisters and I created imaginary lands and kingdoms in our much-loved woods.

One afternoon when I was seven or eight, one of my older sisters and I set out to a favorite playing spot deep in the woods: "Fairyland," a place of lichen-covered boulders, giant maples and elms, and a small stream. As we played, dusk pushed long shadows across our play kingdom until we didn't recognize the way out. We felt confused and disoriented, and one of us said, "We're lost!"

My father's wise words crept into my frightened thoughts: "If you are ever lost, stay right where you are and don't move." Not cold, but shivering with fear, we sat down and waited, knowing Mom would eventually miss us for dinner, and that she and Dad would come looking for us. It was pitch dark before we saw flashlight beams searching between the trees and heard their yells for us. There were hugs and kisses and tears, and our parents held fast to our grimy hands on the walk home.

I'm sure hugs and kisses and tears greeted young Jesus when His parents finally found Him after three days of searching for their "lost" son. (Keep in mind, *He* was never lost; His parents just had to find Him.) After every lead as to His whereabouts turned out to be a false start, can't you imagine their anxious question, "But where can He *be*?" The last place they thought of looking was the temple, never mind among the teachers there, where He was asking and answering questions.

The questions He asked showed wisdom, but even more, He understood the answers the first time through! He wouldn't need a remedial class in law, He "got it" immediately. Jesus had no learning curve.

When Mary and Joseph were searching for their son, they were undoubtedly obsessed with finding Him. They weren't about to give up. Likewise, when twelve-year-old Jesus was learning about the law from the wise teachers, He was obsessed with gaining wisdom. He wasn't going to give up the opportunity to learn. Interestingly, the words He spoke to His parents are the first time we hear His voice. And what does He say? "Didn't you know I had to be in my Father's house?" (v. 49). It's almost as if He's counseling them, "What took you so long to figure out where I was?" I like how the King James Version puts Jesus' words: "I must be about my Father's business."

"Had to be" and "must be" speak of immediacy. They speak of His clear understanding of His current task to absorb all the information He could. Though born perfect and with a sense of destiny in mind, He still had to learn. His biggest learning assignment was to find where He fit in all the laws and regulations and prophecies. No wonder He felt obsessed about gaining wisdom; this was information He needed to accomplish His "Father's business."

*Do we stubbornly set our heels and dig deep into the Word of God when we feel "lost"?*

We have a destiny too as we accomplish our Father's business. But how often do we give up when we feel discouraged or sidetracked? Do we stubbornly set our heels and dig deep into the Word of God when we feel "lost"? Do we feel that same sense of urgency and immediacy as Mary and Joseph and young Jesus when we study God's Word? When we love the Lord with all of our mind, we "must be about [our] Father's business"—getting lost in the business of gaining wisdom from God's Word.

DRAWING CLOSER TODAY

*Thank you, Lord, that your business is mine, and my business is yours. I pray that you will give me a sense of urgency and the willpower not to give up if I ever feel lost or separated from you.*

# STRENGTH

*When the time of their purification according to the Law of Moses had been completed, Joseph and Mary took [Jesus] to Jerusalem to present him to the Lord. . . .*

*The parents brought in the child Jesus to do for him what the custom of the Law required. . . .*

*When Joseph and Mary had done everything required by the Law of the Lord . . .*

*Every year his parents went to Jerusalem for the Feast of the Passover.*

LUKE 2:22, 27, 39, 41

If there is one recurrent theme in the Old Testament, it is obedience versus disobedience. Over and over we read about blatant disobedience. The Israelites alone ignored God's commands, turned their backs on His laws, and denied His character.

That is why, I believe, the New Testament—the books of redemption and lifestyle choices—starts with *obedience*. The gospels of Matthew and Luke each relay the upright and obedient nature of Joseph and Mary. Mary was chosen as Jesus' mother because she was "highly favored" by God (Luke 1:28). His favor was upon her because she had been faithful to favor the Lord above all else. God handpicked her because she held the needed depth of strength-love to be obedient to Him and His laws. Plus, her obedience would extend to raising her son according to the same laws to which she and Joseph were subject. She took the Law of God seriously. She knew to whom she was answerable.

Before the words were even written, Mary put into practice Paul's words from Ephesians 4:1: "Live a life worthy of the calling you have received." What a calling Mary had! But she had already proven that she could and would live a life worthy of the calling, simply by her past obedience.

I wonder if Mary felt qualified for the job the Lord had entrusted to her. This was her firstborn. Our firstborn children tend to be our "trial models." By numbers two, three, or four we feel much more confident in the parenting role. She had no choice but to rely heavily on prayer and the Father's wisdom.

What kind of prayers did she pray for Jesus and for herself? Selfless prayers. Read that again: *selfless*, not selfish. Selfless prayers are like the prayer "Yet not as I will, but as you will" (Matthew 26:39). Who prayed those words? Christ himself.

My mother is involved in a prayer group with several other women. They are the "Beyond Ourselves" prayer group.

Their focus is just what their name says; they pray for the greater circle of life outside their own small circle. That doesn't mean they don't pray for their families and loved ones, but it means they have a global outlook, with the intent of a heavenly impact. They pray selflessly, for God's will, not necessarily their own.

*They have a global outlook, with the intent of a heavenly impact. They pray selflessly, for God's will, not necessarily their own.*

What is required to pray selflessly? The book of Colossians gives us an answer: "Set your hearts on things above, where Christ is seated at the right hand of God. Set your minds on things above" (3:1–2). Set our hearts and minds. Hold them fast in the heavenly realm. This is where the strength of our love for God gives us the power to set and hold our hearts and minds on God's mind and His will. Mary showed the strength of her love for God by obedience to what He instructed her personally to do, plus obedience to the Law of Moses. We too can show the same strength of love for our Lord by obedience to Him and His Word.

What an advantage we have with the New Testament as a guide for how to be obedient: it could well carry the subtitle "Lifestyles of the Rich in the Word and Famous in God's Sight." Let's pray for hearts and minds held fast to God's Word and a desire to be true to it.

DRAWING CLOSER TODAY

*Thank you, Lord, for the heavenly impact of prayers launched unselfishly. I know that when you entrust me with a heavy calling, I can trust you to give me the strength to respond obediently with selfless prayer.*

TO KNOW HIM AS

# WONDERFUL COUNSELOR

Our children are indeed our teachers. This couldn't be more true than in Jesus' relationship with His mother. He came into the world with a foretold title of "Wonderful Counselor," and in His prime years He proved himself worthy of this title in all He said and did.

His wisdom is what counsels us. Counselor is what we need to know Him as when we are confused or hurt or when life just doesn't make sense. And do you know what? Our lives separate from Christ will *never* make sense. We can't make sense out of a half-developed picture. Only the Lord's counsel can reveal to us the defined edges of His loving will.

*Who is "on center" in your life?*

As your heart follows God, will you trust in His wise counsel and then release to Him what you don't understand?

Memory Verse:
*Now we see but a poor reflection as in a mirror; then we shall see face to face. Now I know in part; then I shall know fully, even as I am fully known.*

1 CORINTHIANS 13:12

# 3

# THE SCEPTER OF GRACE:

## *Loving Him in Fear*

TO KNOW HIM AS

## *FAITHFUL*

READ: ESTHER 3–8

# HEART

*There was great mourning among the Jews,*
*with fasting, weeping and wailing. Many lay*
*in sackcloth and ashes. When Esther's maids*
*and eunuchs came and told her about*
*Mordecai, she was in great distress.*

ESTHER 4:3–4

I stood in a room of about one hundred children, ranging in age from two to eighteen years. My back to a wall, observing the children interact and behave so . . . well, childlike, I felt my heart breaking. Here before me were children with insulin-dependent diabetes—my then eight-year-old son among them. Trying not to let them see the tears about to slip from the edges of my eyes, I felt akin to the other parents around the room. I knew they had the same overpowering feelings of heartbreak over these innocent children who did not deserve such a devastating disease. At the time I was a relatively new member to the community of parents whose children have diabetes, but I had already experienced the same pain and mourning.

I've come to learn that, for a divine reason, God puts us in communities of people where we share similar experiences. It may be because we have things of faith to share with them. It may also be because we have things to learn from them. We may not want to be part of these sometimes-scary communities, but He has a plan for us there.

Such was the case for Esther, who found herself queen of the Israelite people, elevated above her Jewish heritage. But she was still a Jewess at heart.

She responded with "great distress" to Mordecai's weeping and mourning over the edict for the death of all the Jews, issued by her impulsive husband, King Xerxes. Her heart was broken. Her grief wasn't only for her dear Uncle Mordecai but also for the entire Jewish nation.

She faced a choice: she could turn her back on her people, including her uncle and the rest of her adopted family, or she could intervene. How could her heart respond to such a quandary? She loved her uncle. She loved her heritage. Though her husband-king didn't even know she was a Jew, she was proud of her roots.

Interestingly, Esther is the only book in the Bible that doesn't mention God by name. But His presence is palpable. The response of Mordecai and the Jews with their traditional mourning routine, proves that they held the Lord God and His laws in the highest regard.

Esther's heart-love for her family—and her God and His laws—is what motivated her to go before the king, risking certain death, to express her concern and fear for God's chosen people: "I will go to the king, even though it is against the law. And if I perish, I perish" (4:16). What does this tell us? Esther's love for God and His plan for her life within that community was greater than her fear of death.

> *Esther's love for God and His plan for her life within that community was greater than her fear of death.*

Few of us will ever experience a decision so profound. Hers was a decision to express her love for God over her fear of man, her husband, and the law of the land.

Do we, *could we*, if put to the test, show our heart of love for the Lord to be greater than our need for approval from people? How strong is our sense of self-preservation in our faith?

I once read that our personal faith-based passion shows in our willingness to die for the cause. What are we willing to die for? Even more, what are we willing to *live* for?

## DRAWING CLOSER TODAY

*Lord, I want my heart to be true to you in all things. Even if I'm never challenged with a life-or-death situation as Esther was, I pray that I will always put my love for you first—in my life, my home, and my community.*

# SOUL

*All the king's officials and the people of the royal provinces know that for any man or woman who approaches the king in the inner court without being summoned the king has but one law: that he be put to death. The only exception to this is for the king to extend the gold scepter to him and spare his life. . . .*

*When [King Xerxes] saw Queen Esther standing in the court, he was pleased with her and held out to her the gold scepter that was in his hand. So Esther approached and touched the tip of the scepter.*

ESTHER 4:11; 5:2

Why do you think an invitation from the king was necessary before a person could approach his throne? It wasn't a personal space issue; distance offered protection. Like a

CIA agent who always faces doorways and keeps his back to a wall, the king ordered a moat of space around himself for safety and to ensure that all his subjects stayed honest and fearful of him. The king's throne in the inner court awarded him the honor and respect that he deserved.

What was the significance of the inner court? In the king's palace, the court is where he sat publicly before his officials, yet was protected from the crowds. There's a symbolic parallel between the king's inner court and the "inner courts" that are spoken of in Psalms. Our inner court is where we are "public" before the Lord, open and vulnerable, yet our souls are protected from public view. The interior of our souls is where our Lord dwells within us. We enter the inner court of the Lord through prayer, sometimes through agonizing, put-every-other-distraction-aside prayer. As Psalm 84:2 says, "My soul yearns, even faints, for the courts of the Lord; my heart and my flesh cry out for the living God." It's as if the psalmist was feeling banished from the inner courts of the Lord, and his soul felt desperate to be back in God's presence.

Perhaps Esther felt a bit the same way. Certainly she was frightened about going to the king without an invitation. Do you hear a bit of frustration in her words: "But thirty days have passed since I was called to go to the king"? (4:11). She had been keeping track since her last visit. She missed her king—her husband (this also speaks of her sexuality). She wanted to be with him, to spend time with him, to talk to him. But she hadn't been summoned in a month.

With deep courage and conviction, yet humbled by a sense of personal sacrifice, she does approach the king. And what is his response? He is *pleased* with her. Maybe he admires her tenacity and bravery. Maybe her beauty has once again captivated his heart. Maybe he's simply happy to see her because he loves her. Then he extends the gold scepter. What does that gold scepter represent? *Grace*. It meant, "You are pardoned from death."

Whew! What relief!

In our lives, the Lord has a perpetual scepter of grace extended to us. Unlike Esther, we don't have to be summoned. We don't have to wait to be asked to approach our King. We don't have to be fearful of entering the "inner courts."

On the day Jesus died on the cross to save our souls from sin, the gold scepter of forgiveness and grace became a permanent staff for us to grasp. His scepter of grace for us will never be withdrawn. It's held out day and night, week after week, month after month, year after year. Why? Because our Lord is always happy to see us. He always loves us. He's always glad to spend time with us. He is continually faithful to welcome us into His presence.

*On the day Jesus died on the cross to save our souls from sin, the gold scepter of forgiveness and grace became a permanent staff for us to grasp.*

Our soul-love for the Lord rests securely in His scepter of grace. We know we can trust Him with all of our love because He will not withdraw His grace from us. We can enter His inner court with confidence and assurance that we are wanted there, and He is pleased to see us there.

"Let us then approach the throne of grace with confidence, so that we may receive mercy and find grace to help us in our time of need" (Hebrews 4:16).


DRAWING CLOSER TODAY

*Lord, thank you that I don't have to wait for you to call to me to enter your presence. Thank you that I can come to you with all the love in my soul, knowing your love and grace for me are eternal.*

# MIND

*Do not think that because you are in the
king's house you alone of all the Jews will
escape. . . . And who knows but that you
have come to royal position for such a time
as this?*

ESTHER 4:13–14

D o you feel like royalty? I certainly don't. I don't
get up in the morning and don my diamond-
studded tiara. I'm not served my morning
coffee on a gold tray. I don't pass along the
cleaning supplies to an attendant. No, I'm more likely to pull
on my barn clothes, leaving my hair unbrushed, and trip to
the kitchen for my coffee in a chipped mug. And I definitely
clean my own bathrooms.

Yet the Bible says that we *are* royalty. "But you are a chosen people, a royal priesthood, a holy nation, a people belonging to God" (1 Peter 2:9). And Romans 8:17 says, "We are

heirs—heirs of God and co-heirs with Christ." Even in my less-than-royal garb, I am royalty in God's family. He may not adorn me with exterior riches, but He's given me something far more precious: an abiding place in His family.

Within His family, we have responsibilities. Just as my children each have their daily chores, in God's family we have jobs to do too. We aren't excluded because of our age, gender, race, or size.

> *Esther understood her position: to serve the Lord as her high priest in the position He had called her to by serving His people.*

Such were the thoughts of Mordecai when his words sent a convicting arrow through Esther's defenses. Read the above Scripture again. In essence, Uncle Mordecai was saying, "You may be royalty in the king's house, but you are part of God's family first. Remember your roots. Maybe the Lord has put you in the palace for this very reason: to stand up for God's chosen people."

It would have been easy for Esther to turn her back. She could have rationalized it away: "I'm above this. After all, I am *the queen!*" But she didn't. Instead, she responded with humility of mind. She knew in her heart and in her intellect that Mordecai was right. Esther understood her position: to serve the Lord as her high priest in the position He had called her to by serving His people. Her royal position within her husband's house was ancillary.

When we are motivated by humility of mind, our mind-love for Christ shows. It's so easy to think we are "above" something. It's so easy to convince ourselves that we've "earned" the right to be excused from serving in the trenches of Christianity. We think our knowledge of Scripture, our teaching Bible classes, or our long-held faith means that we don't have to "get dirty" for the Lord anymore.

I'm reminded of a man in my church who, on a domestic mission trip, helped lay a new sewer line for a poor family. As you can imagine, laying a new sewer line meant dismantling the *old* sewer line: stinky, disgusting labor. I'm told that this leader in our church, a Christian for decades, did not complain. He humbly got dirty for God. I don't know his inner thoughts, but I do know his outward actions left an impression on some young-in-the-Lord people.

That's humility of mind. That's loving the Lord God with enough of our minds to extradite pride from our thoughts and respond to the royal position God has called us to. That's being selfless and not elevating ourselves to a self-imposed position of authority or significance or self-importance.

"If anyone has material possessions and sees his brother in need but has no pity on him, how can the love of God be in him? Dear children, let us not love with words or tongue but with actions and truth" (1 John 3:17–18).

## DRAWING CLOSER TODAY

*Lord, forgive me for the times that self-importance has dominated my mind. Help me to have humility of mind as I learn to love you more. Teach me to lovingly serve you in whatever position you call me to.*

# STRENGTH

*Go, gather together all the Jews who are in*
*Susa, and fast for me. Do not eat or drink*
*for three days, night or day. I and my maids*
*will fast as you do.*

ESTHER 4:16

everal years ago a family crisis held my mind hostage.
Awake and asleep, the thoughts of this heart-
stopping, life-changing situation dominated my
every attempt at normalcy. Activities that I usually
attended to with energy and enthusiasm were left unfinished
or entirely undone. I couldn't follow a conversation for more
than a few seconds. I had no strength in my mind or body to
do anything. The problem transfixed my concentration, like a
bad song repeating a tune and words in my head that I
couldn't shut off.

I can't help but think that this is how Esther felt when
she heard that her entire nation was to be killed by the sword.

*How absolutely devastating.* In twenty-first-century terms, that would be like the entire Christian population of our nation being wiped out at the command of a ruthless president. Sends a shiver down your spine, doesn't it?

Esther wasn't immobilized with the knowledge of this impending devastation, though. Instead, it stirred to action her strength-love for God and her people. She immediately answered Mordecai's plea for intercession by calling for a three-day-and-night fast. And she didn't exclude herself from the fast. She knew the importance of setting an example for her fellow Jews.

She and all the Jews of Susa (and even her maids, who likely weren't Jewish) put all their strength into the fast. Much the way I felt about my family crisis, nothing else mattered anymore. The fasting Jews put aside everything to tend to the business of fasting and petitioning the Lord for deliverance.

During those three days, could Esther imagine the scene that might unfold as her people lay dying—the cries and the blood? When she saw these things in her mind's eye, did she squeeze her eyes shut tight and pray with more determination than ever before?

Esther knew what was at stake. An entire nation of lives literally depended on her. She also felt keenly aware of the potential cost personally. She faced death no matter what: for petitioning the king without being summoned, for the fact that she was a Jew, or through self-hatred if she failed to speak up. Talk about being stuck between a rock and a hard place! Her *only* option was to fast and pray. Fasting and praying was *all* she could do. Racing through villages on horseback, asking the Jews to flee, wouldn't have worked. Trying to hide them would be impossible. Telling them to rally the troops and fight back was not feasible. She could expend no energy on any plan.

The truth is, her inactivity showed the greatest amount of strength. Her strength for three days and nights of prayer came from her inner-held beliefs and confidence in the Lord.

> *Nothing shows strength of love for the Lord like relying on Him exclusively.*

Nothing shows strength of love for the Lord like relying on Him exclusively. When we love Him full-strength, nothing else matters, nothing else occupies our minds. During a fast, all external resources for strength (i.e., food) are stopped so that our strength to carry on can come only from inner-held resources. For Esther, and for us, that inner-held resource is our love for the Lord. He is the one who sustains us.

Hold tightly to that love for Him. It is the only option we have when a crisis threatens to strip us of all that we hold dear.

DRAWING CLOSER TODAY

*Lord, prepare me for a call on my life that may require me to respond with full-strength love for you. I don't want to react in fear or anger or haste. Remind me to always put all of me into petitioning all of you for answers.*

TO KNOW HIM AS

# FAITHFUL

Esther saw through to the end the call the Lord placed on her life. At the end of her season of fear and uncertainty for her people, what did she discover? Something I suspect she already knew: God hears. God cares. God is faithful.

Faithfulness means He is full of faith to give. His faithfulness to us never runs out or gets used up. He's not like us, where our wells of good intentions run dry. He is enduring in His love, sufficient in His provision, honest in His intent.

*Who is "on center" in your life?*

Will you pray through to the end whatever fear you may be dealing with in your life, knowing that the Lord will faithfully walk the way with you?

Memory Verse:

*"So do not fear, for I am with you; do not be dismayed, for I am your God. I will strengthen you and help you; I will uphold you with my righteous right hand."*

ISAIAH 41:10

# 4

# THE RICHES OF THE POOR:

*Loving Him When It Costs Everything*

TO KNOW HIM AS

## PROVIDER

READ: MARK 12:38–44

# HEART

*Jesus sat down opposite where the offerings*
*were put and watched the crowd putting*
*their money into the temple treasury. Many*
*rich people threw in large amounts.*

MARK 12:41

J esus is the master of object lessons. Little did a poor widow know she was about to become the subject of a lesson about how two coins changed the disciples'—and our—understanding about generosity and sacrifice.

Jesus had just been teaching at the temple courts about pride and sacrifice. He sat down, perhaps for a breather, and quietly watched people step up and drop their money into the temple treasury. He sat alone. His disciples had wandered a little way off.

Silently up the steps comes a widow lady, presumably old. She meekly drops in two coins and then shuffles away. We don't know her thoughts; we don't even hear her speak. We don't know if she knew that Jesus was right there, or if she even knew who He was. Yet she is given a distinct place in the Bible. Her actions have not gone unnoticed.

Did her offering make a difference? Financially, probably not. To the Lord, that was the whole point. The offering wasn't about money. It was about the woman's heart. Her offering made a difference because it was given with a pure heart.

What is a pure heart? A heart without ulterior motive. A heart that isn't interested in who is watching. A heart that is unblemished by selfishness or conceit or pride. A heart that is interested only in being seen as loving the Lord God. That's purity.

*Purity is birthed in us and grown under duress. Purity doesn't take up residence in our hearts because we are guiltless; it comes to stay because we are guilty.*

We can't wake up one day and simply *decide* to have a pure heart. It's one of the hardest traits to consistently live. David said in Psalm 51:10, "Create in me a pure heart, O God, and renew a steadfast spirit within me." We can't do it on our own. As David suggests, it's created in us by opportunities to consistently choose purity. Purity is birthed in us and grown under duress. Purity doesn't take up residence in our hearts because we are guiltless; it comes to stay because we are guilty. We wouldn't understand or desire purity if we didn't have marred hearts.

When Jesus watched the widow give her small offering He saw only purity. She was only one woman, inconspicuous among the "many wealthy" in the crowd. In contrast, what did He see in the wealthy? A lack of humility and sacrifice.

What does this say to our twenty-first-century hearts? Some of us may be wealthy, others near poverty. Most of us are probably in the middle. In all our giving, whether it's money, time, resources, or ourselves, we show our love for the Lord when we give out of a pure heart. Second Corinthians 9:6–7 reminds us of the paradox of a miserly heart versus a generous heart. "Remember this: Whoever sows sparingly will also reap sparingly, and whoever sows generously will also reap generously. Each man should give what he has decided in his heart to give, not reluctantly or under compulsion, for God loves a cheerful giver." It's not the amount that matters, but the pure heart attitude behind the giving that's important.

Are our hearts "sparing" with a miserly attitude in our giving? Or do we have pure hearts so full of love for the Lord that we generously and cheerfully offer back to Him all that He's given us?

## DRAWING CLOSER TODAY

*Lord, you do know my heart. You know the degree of purity with which I bring my offerings to you. I pray that if there resides in me any pride in my giving, that it would be replaced with humility. I pray that if there is any hesitation in my giving, that it would be replaced with joyful liberty.*

# SOUL

*But a poor widow came and put in two very
small copper coins, worth only a fraction of
a penny.*

MARK 12:42

I remember hearing a story when I was a child that left an impression on me. It went something like this:

As the church offering plate was handed up and down the pews one Sunday morning, a little boy in the back row fidgeted and brooded. His agitation grew as the plate made its way closer and closer to his pew. His mother placed a firm hand on his leg and told him to settle down. When his fidgeting turned into standing up and sitting down, his mother crossly hissed at him, "What is bothering you?"

"I have nothing to put in the offering plate!" he choked.

Even as the words left his mouth, the plate started down his row. Then all of a sudden a smile lit his face. When his mother started to pass the plate past her young son, he grabbed it, set it on the pew, and promptly sat in it!

"I don't have any money to put in, but I want to put *me* in!" he declared.

I still remember hearing this because the message I took away was simple enough for a child to understand: An offering to the Lord isn't just about money—it's about offering all of what I've got, even if that all is *me*.

> *We can become minimalists of ourselves. It means dropping into the Lord's treasury the last vestiges of our own will.*

The poor widow may well have wished she could jump into the temple treasury. Though bodily she didn't, in effect she did offer her whole self. Similar to our culture, much wealth surrounded her, but out of necessity she lived a minimalist life. It meant there was lots of room in her soul for the Lord to work His will in her life. The less there was of her and her will, the more room there was for Him.

That's not to say we should all go and sell our homes and become minimalists in where and how we live, but it does mean we can become minimalists of *ourselves*. It means dropping into the Lord's treasury the last vestiges of our own will. The widow's will may have whispered in her ear, *"This small amount doesn't matter. Nobody is going to notice if you don't give these coins."* In our lives, our will may say, *"I'll hold on to this one little piece of treasure; it's too insignificant to matter to the Lord."* But, do you know what? It does matter, because our soul and our will are no longer ours when we come before the Lord's treasury.

The poor widow can't have known how those two small coins would make a difference in a multitude of people's lives—yours and mine included. It was such a small occurrence, of no note to anyone but Christ, yet it is detailed in the Bible. It makes you think, doesn't it?

Those two coins have a weighty significance. What did they represent to her, and to us? Until they slid into the treasury chest, they were mere bits of money. But upon the "clink, clink" of their hitting other coins, the first coin represented obedience, and the other trust. They were all she had to offer: obedience and trust. This was indeed all she had to live on. She had nothing else.

With her offering she emptied herself of any earthly value. At the same time her value in heaven multiplied. How? She walked away from the temple treasury with more than what she brought: faith. Deep soul-faith. Faith that the Lord would provide, faith that she had done the right thing. Faith that the obedience and trust she dropped in would multiply into something useful for the Lord.

It's easy to give out of our abundance, much harder to give out of what we *don't* have. If we don't have something, how can we offer it? Like the little boy who offered himself, that's all the Lord is after. Out of our brokenness, our spiritual poverty, our lack of human riches, we can simply give ourselves.

Like the widow's offering, our "small coins" are obedience and trust. Can we obediently offer what we don't have to the Lord? That's part of what loving Him with all of our soul means—offering our soul depleted of our own will so He can refill it with faith.

DRAWING CLOSER TODAY

*Lord, I offer my will to you today. I know how it can hinder me from offering a soul empty of all but love for you. I pray that as I choose to act in obedience and trust, you will fill my soul with faith.*

# MIND

*As he taught, Jesus said, "Watch out for the teachers of the law. They like to walk around in flowing robes and be greeted in the marketplaces, and have the most important seats in the synagogues and the places of honor at banquets."*

*Jesus sat down opposite the place where the offerings were put and watched the crowd. . . .*

*Calling his disciples to him . . .*

MARK 12:38, 41, 43

After nearly nineteen years of marriage, I know how my husband's mind works. I understand the contours of the track on which his mind travels, the shifts and bends of his personal psyche. He knows my mind pretty well too. After living with each other for so long, we can almost predict what the other is thinking . . . almost.

Actually, it's probably good that we can't fully read each other's minds. Since we're sinners and think sinful thoughts, I certainly don't want my every thought broadcast to the person on earth whom I love the most.

I may be able to hide some of my thoughts from my husband, but the sad truth is that the one I love in heaven more than anything on earth can read my mind.

Christ is as familiar with our minds as we are. Embarrassingly so. Because He *knows* our minds. He does fathom our deepest thoughts and the nuances of our every action. Are we motivated by selfish ambition (Philippians 2:3), or wholehearted devotion and a willing mind (1 Chronicles 28:9)?

When Jesus warned the disciples to "watch out for the teachers of the law," He was telling His co-laborers that He could read the teachers' minds, and He knew the depravity that resided there. Watching the teachers of the law mindlessly throw their money into the treasury, He saw how their minds swelled with self-importance, greed, pride, and superiority.

What's wrong with these attitudes and traits? They are sinful because they are *human-motivated*. The teachers were out to get a response, a reaction for themselves. They thought they could impress their own kind.

Maybe the disciples nodded their heads in understanding of this important warning lesson. Perhaps they formed a small circle to discuss the new knowledge while the Lord sat down to silently watch the treasury. Unnoticed, the widow steps up and drops in her two coins. What does Christ do? "Calling his disciples to him . . ." He wanted to now call their attention to another mind He just saw: one of humility, obedience, trust, and sacrifice. The widow wasn't concerned with people's approval. She didn't let the possibility of thoughts of embarrassment or shame prevent her from acting on God's prompting. No one was watching her, only God. The Lord saw in her heart and mind that she knew to whom she was accountable.

Jesus knew her gift was a true sacrifice. That's why He said she had "put more into the treasury than all the others." Not just any *one* of the wealthy people, but more than *all* of the others.

Christ knew a bit about sacrifice. Perhaps He knew the widow's offering was a small reflection of His own impending, death-defying sacrifice. Emotional or physical pain is often part of sacrifice. It has to hurt.

As we love the Lord God with more of our mind, we understand the need for sacrificial giving. Our sacrifices must cost us something. When King David built an altar on Araunah's threshing floor to sacrifice burnt offerings so a plague on Israel

*As we love the Lord God with more of our mind, we understand the need for sacrificial giving. Our sacrifices must cost us something.*

would be lifted, he insisted on paying for the land, though Araunah said he could have it for free. "But the king replied to Araunah, 'No, I insist on paying you for it. I will not sacrifice to the Lord my God burnt offerings that cost me nothing'" (2 Samuel 24:24).

In our daily planners, our monthly calendars, and our checkbooks, it may look as though we have nothing to offer: time, energy, or money. But loving the Lord God with abandon, as the widow did, costs us all we have. As King David demonstrated to Araunah, we can't offer a sacrifice if we have sacrificed nothing for the offering.


DRAWING CLOSER TODAY

*Lord, my mind has a hard time absorbing this truth of sacrifice. Yet, I know emptying myself of myself is what loving you more fully requires. I offer my will and my mind for you to have as an empty vessel.*

# STRENGTH

*But she, out of her poverty, put in*
*everything—all she had to live on.*

MARK 12:44

A friend of mine once said, "Loss and grief are like trying to eat an elephant with a plastic fork." Loss feels insurmountable. It leaves us weak-kneed. Yet there's a need to internalize it and ruminate on what the loss means to us personally. Pushing loss away at arm's length holds God's healing ministry at a distance too. There is no way to experience the relief found in Him if we don't allow the overwhelming pain first.

The pain will have a useful end. In *My Utmost for His Highest*, Oswald Chambers wrote, "God never has museums" (May 15). Nothing is useless to the Lord. Our lives cannot be antiquated. Where we feel used or weak is where His daily grace renews us. Paul understood this philosophy when he wrote,

"Three times I pleaded with the Lord to take [a thorn in my flesh] away from me. But he said to me, 'My grace is sufficient for you, for my power is made perfect in weakness'" (2 Corinthians 12:8–9).

*Where we feel used or weak is where His daily grace renews us.*

The poor widow knew about loss. Her husband was dead. It's implied that she had no family. Maybe she had a "thorn in her flesh" of poverty or sorrow or loneliness or unrealized hopes and dreams. Maybe each morning she rolled out of her simple mat bed and faced that gray elephant of loss.

When she tossed in the last remains of any personal possession, the widow was weak in human terms—she was literally down to nothing. But she was the strongest she'd ever been in her relationship with God. She was willing to be weak so that God could be strong in her. Yet her weakness was her greatest strength too.

It's a hard-to-understand dichotomy: the weaker we are in ourselves, the stronger our love is for the Lord. Our greatest strength is the weakness we know exists apart from a side-by-side alliance with and dependence on Him.

My ninety-five-year-old grandmother, legally blind and failing rapidly, made her final earthly move to a nursing home not far from my mother's house. Several years before they had walked the bridge of reversed parent/child roles. Not an easy transition, but a necessary one. Once a vibrant and fiercely independent woman, now my grandmother found herself completely dependent on my mom. The weaker she grew, the deeper her attachment to my mother. As childlikeness claimed my grandmother's body and mind, my mother became her eyes, ears, and voice. The strength of their mutual love was knit out of my grandmother's weakness.

This was a concept I needed to understand, and how like our faithful Lord to provide a human parallel to a lesson He wants us to know. As I observed in the relationship between my mother and her mother, I learned that between Christ and us a mutual love is woven out of our weakness and His strength. We are woven into the tapestry of His design. Alone, a single thread is easily ripped, but laced into His support we are strong *in Him and through Him*. He stands in the place for us when we are weak. His strength fills the void left by our weaknesses, whether those weaknesses are physical, emotional, or spiritual.

The King James Version of Mark 12:42 says that the widow put in "two mites"—a very small form of currency. I like to think of her offering as her "might." She gave her strength in love and obedience to the Lord's treasury. She did not want to withhold it. Why? Because He did not require her to be strong. Nor does He require strength in us. Why would we then need Him? The only strength He wants in us is a conviction of remaining weak so His strength can prevail.

DRAWING CLOSER TODAY

> *Thank You, Lord, that you have no requirement of us to be strong in our own "might." Thank you for the weaknesses in my life, where I can lean more heavily on you. I love the strength I have in you. Be the "stronghold of my life" (Psalm 27:1).*

TO KNOW HIM AS

# PROVIDER

How will the poor widow be most remembered? Her epitaph could read: "When nothing meant everything and everything meant nothing."

When we are emptied out of our will and self the Lord has the greatest opportunity to be our provider. But don't sell Him short. He won't only provide our material needs. He's the provider of grace, hope, peace, and life.

He bought us for a price: His life. It cost Him all to be our all. I, too, can invest all of me in that kind of holy economy. How about you?

*Who is "on center" in your life?*

Will you lay down your all—your heart, your will, your mind—at the foot of the cross so He can be your one and only provider?

Memory Verse:
*For if, by the trespass of the one man, death reigned through that one man, how much more will those who receive God's abundant provision of grace and of the gift of righteousness reign in life through the one man, Jesus Christ.*

ROMANS 5:17

# 5

# THE STONES OF FAITH:

*Loving Him Unto Death*

TO KNOW HIM AS

*ALMIGHTY GOD*

READ: ACTS 6–7

# HEART

*But our fathers refused to obey [Moses].*
*Instead they rejected him and in their hearts*
*turned back to Egypt.*

ACTS 7:39

The story is told of a man walking down the street on a dark night. He's familiar with the street, but it's unlit, and he suddenly falls into a hole. A bit bruised, he brushes himself off and scampers out of the hole to continue on his way, a slight limp in his step. The next night he's walking down the same unlit street. Again, he walks right into the hole. This time he's a little more bruised, and it takes him a few more minutes to crawl out before he hobbles on his way. The third night he's again walking down the same dark street. This time he remembers there's a hole, and he catches himself just before stepping in, but twists his ankle in the process. Limping away, he's grateful he missed the hole. The fourth night the man is out for a walk again. Only this night . . . he walks down a different street.

How like us. How many times do we fall into the same hole before we realize we need to take a different route? The hole may be the pit of depression, or it might be the jagged-edged hollow of pride. Maybe it's the abyss of fear.

These threatening holes can be bondages in our lives. They hold us captive, they ensnare our legs when we are trying to walk with the Lord. Like the alcoholic who after a night of bingeing swears he'll never return to the bar, the very next night finds himself on the same street, pulling open the heavy door of the same bar. The will of his heart wasn't as strong as the familiar addiction.

There's a similarity in the talk the deacon Stephen gave to the Sanhedrin, comparing them to the wandering, stubborn Israelites. The Israelites disobeyed Moses, and their "hearts turned back to Egypt." Why would their hearts turn back to Egypt? It had been a place of bondage, a place of slavery. Why, in heaven's name,

*When we choose Christ as Savior of our lives, He saves us from our lives.*

would their hearts want to return to such a life? Because it was familiar. Because wandering around in the desert felt hard with all its uncertainties. At least in Egypt, they knew what to expect—even if the working conditions were deplorable.

Are we much different? Don't we, too, return to the comfort of familiarity because we know the way?

But when Christ sets us free from bondages, we don't need to keep returning to what is behind us. When we choose

Christ as Savior of our lives, He saves us from our lives. Our faith-walk takes us down a new street.

Stephen tried to challenge the Sanhedrin to repent. The Hebrew word for repentance translates "to turn back." This is a good kind of turning back—not turning back to the old way—but a return to God's way. He wanted them to recognize their sins and turn back to godly lives. He knew they were in perpetual bondage to the past sins of their forefathers, yet they knowingly continued down the same path.

A heart full of love for Christ means we've put our trust in Him to lead us safely past our bondages. With Him, freedom is what becomes familiar, not a return over and over to what is behind us. Yes, it may feel as though there is uncertainty in the newfound freedom. But our certainty always lies in the Lord's holy Word: "Then your light will break forth like the dawn, and your healing will quickly appear; then your righteousness will go before you, and the glory of the Lord will be your rear guard. Then you will call, and the Lord will answer; you will cry for help, and he will say: Here am I" (Isaiah 58:8–9).

DRAWING CLOSER TODAY

*Lord, you and I both know the paths I walk on with familiar holes. I pray that today I will let you lead me down a new road.*

# SOUL

*You stiff-necked people, with uncircumcised
hearts and ears! You are just like your
fathers: You always resist the Holy Spirit!*

ACTS 7:51

hat did Stephen mean when he accused the
Sanhedrin of having uncircumcised hearts?
Let's consider what circumcision meant to
the Israelites' souls in the Jewish faith.
When God established the covenant of circumcision, it
was meant as a mark of ownership. It meant their souls belonged to the Lord God. Genesis 17:13 says, "My covenant in
your flesh is to be an everlasting covenant." The promised
multiple descendants of Abraham's family would be recognized as the family of God's chosen people, by the cutting of
their skin. Imagine telling grown men that this needed to be
done so they would be known as God's extended family. Can't
you picture the men's grimaces and cringes? But, of course,

they obeyed. To possibly be left out from God's promises was unthinkable.

Similarly, in Exodus 21:2–6 (interestingly, right after the listing of the Ten Commandments), a law is detailed concerning how to release a Hebrew servant after six years of labor. But if the servant *wanted* to continue under his master's rule, he could choose to do so. The master then took the servant to a doorpost, laid his ear against it, and pierced his ear with an awl. "Then he will be his servant for life" (v. 6).

In both cases the pain and cutting of flesh proved ownership: their body and soul belonged to someone else.

> I wanted my commitment inside to be seen outside.

A number of years ago, I chose to take the Exodus 21:2–6 verses literally. I wanted there to be an outward sign of my soul belonging to my Lord. My ears had already been pierced once when I was a teenager, but I had each ear pierced a second time. Some could say I had the second holes done in response to a trend. But I know my heart's intent: I wanted my commitment inside to be seen outside. I wanted the second hole to be a sign of obedience and a mark of ownership. Like the Hebrew servants in the Old Testament, I opted for the choice of *staying* a servant with my Master. I wanted to serve Him for life.

When Stephen talked to the Sanhedrin, he pointed out to them that they displayed no outward behavior that marked their ownership in God's family. He accused them of being stubborn, disobedient, disrespectful, and self-minded. When he addressed them, "You stiff-necked people..." he effectively laid bare their souls: nothing was there. Empty of commitment and void of faith, there was no love for their God or His Word, even though they had been raised on it and exposed to it their entire lives. He was giving them one last option: let your ears and hearts be pierced and recognize the truth of what I'm telling you. In effect, he was screaming at them: "You have not chosen to allow this mark of ownership on your souls, and I fear for what will happen to you!"

The Lord circumcises our heart when we confess and agree to be a part of His family. He pierces our ears so we can better serve Him faithfully. Our flesh is laid bare. By the removal of our flesh—our own instincts—the way opens for God's way. Our soul is exposed as His.

Ask Him to peel away those things in your soul that act as a barrier to loving Him. Is a lack of faith in the way? Have you allowed disrespect for God's holiness to infiltrate your soul?

When we love Him full soul-strength, we should let nothing stand in the way of lining up at His holy doorpost to figuratively get our ears pierced for Him, proclaiming undying loyalty to Him as Master.

DRAWING CLOSER TODAY

*Lord, I would rather have the pain and discomfort that come with the revelation of a circumcised heart and a pierced ear than to squander my soul. My soul longs to fulfill my love for you as your servant for life.*

# MIND

*But they could not stand up against his*
*wisdom or the Spirit by whom he spoke.*
*To this he replied: "Brothers and*
*fathers, listen to me! The God of glory*
*appeared to our father Abraham while he*
*was still in Mesopotamia, before he lived in*
*Haran. . . .*
*After the death of his father, God sent*
*him to this land where you are now living."*

ACTS 6:10; 7:2, 4

tephen was a great historian ... and a frustrated
teacher. He desperately wanted the Sanhedrin to *un-*
*derstand* why he felt they were in the wrong. He truly
cared about their spiritual poverty. Otherwise, he
could have shrugged off their questioning and answered
tersely. But he really wanted them to see the connection between their past heritage and their current actions. To his

great irritation, they wouldn't listen.

Chapter 6, verse 10, says, "They could not stand up against his wisdom." Stephen was indeed an exceptionally wise man. He not only had God-given wisdom but also intelligence. The two combined awarded him a convicting, spirit-filled message about the Jewish heritage. He conveyed the nuances of God's Word; he even quoted actual conversations correctly. That's pretty remarkable. No wonder the Sanhedrin priests couldn't stand up to him. No wonder the more he talked, the more they felt threatened. They were supposed to be the wise men. He was proving himself wiser.

Stephen obviously was anointed with the Holy Spirit for that last sermon of his life. He probably also knew what he was getting himself into. A place he wouldn't get out of alive. Somehow it didn't matter to him. He knew when he spoke the truth he was speaking the Truth.

His conviction of speaking the truth convicts me. How often do we *not* speak the truth because we know what we'll be getting ourselves into? Maybe with a family member or a co-worker we bite our tongues because it's easier not to speak from God's Word.

My husband and I have a contractor friend. As he stood in our barnyard one day, he was commenting, loudly, about our neighbors and their illegal dumping of barn refuse into a wetland. I could see that the neighbors were easily within earshot right across the road. I motioned to the contractor about the people standing *right there* and "shushed" him. He put his fists on his hips, looked across the road and back at me, and yelled, "Well, you can shout the truth!"

Though said without love, his words were true. We *can* shout the truth!

How do we know the truth and when to speak it? That's where God's mind of wisdom enters. When we love God with all our mind, our hope is to think only godly thoughts. If what we are thinking are godly thoughts, then we'll have God's mind to know when to speak and, just as important, when not to speak. Proverbs 12:18–19 says, "Reckless words pierce like a sword, but the tongue of the wise brings healing. Truthful lips endure forever."

> *If we are thinking godly thoughts, then we'll have God's mind to know when to speak and when not to speak.*

Do you feel as though you're not even close to attaining God's wisdom? James tells us that all we have to do is unassumingly ask, "If any of you lacks wisdom, he should ask God, who gives generously to all without finding fault, and it will be given to him" (James 1:5). Then he goes on to clarify godly wisdom: "But the wisdom that comes from heaven is first of all pure; then peace-loving, considerate, submissive, full of mercy and good fruit, impartial and sincere" (3:17). Living with this kind of wisdom is nothing short of a lifestyle of wisdom, which is exactly what loving the Lord God with all your mind means. It's a chosen lifestyle to "think on these things" (see Philippians 4:8).

DRAWING CLOSER TODAY

*Lord, I desire all my thoughts to always be couched in your wisdom. Thank you for the words in James that say I can confidently pray for more wisdom so I can answer always with your Truth.*

# STRENGTH

*But Stephen, full of the Holy Spirit, looked
up to heaven and saw the glory of God, and
Jesus standing at the right hand of God.*

*While they were stoning him, Stephen
prayed, "Lord Jesus, receive my spirit." Then
he fell on his knees.*

ACTS 7:55, 59–60

H ave you ever read a verse in the Bible that you
just didn't understand? When that happens to
me, the passage holds me captive, and I pray
over it, sometimes for weeks, until the Lord
shows me the meaning.

Such was the case with Genesis 3:16, which says, "Your
desire will be for your husband, and he will rule over you."
This verse, located in the middle of the curses set on mankind
because of original sin, simply didn't make sense to me. I
knew that marriage was a partnership, and that sexual desire

for one's husband was a God-given, *good* thing. Why would it be located among the curses?

Several weeks passed while I genuinely prayed for understanding. The answer came in a book I received in the mail that I had not ordered (so like the Lord to answer in such a way). In one small section, this book addressed the very question I had. I finally got it. The "desire" spoken of is for mankind's *approval*. The curse was that a "fear of man" would forever shadow our fear of the Lord.

Don't we find ourselves constantly operating under this curse of trying to please people? I know I do. The problem is that we use our strength in an attempt to appease others instead of pledging undying strength-love for God.

In the previous meditation, we looked at Stephen's wisdom. His wisdom gave him strength to stand up to men. He proved that he had both intelligence and God-given wisdom. How had he developed such godly wisdom? I believe he ascribed to a concept found in Psalm 111:10: "The fear of the Lord is the beginning of wisdom." Stephen was wise because he feared the Lord *first*. He feared the Lord more than he feared people. His fear, love, respect, and honor of the Lord were far greater than his fear of what men could do to him.

The more Stephen talked to the Sanhedrin, trying to reason with them, the angrier they got. Not just angry—murderously rage-filled. It's at this point that we wonder if Stephen knew just how far he was pushing them. Their anger actually seemed to give him strength to keep hammering them with conviction after conviction. The more they resisted, the less he felt fearful of what they could or would do. His fate was pretty obvious, but he figured he had absolutely nothing to lose. He would not and could not weaken before men, because his strength was in his fear of the Lord.

*He would not and could not weaken before men, because his strength was in his fear of the Lord.*

One of the most remarkable insights about Stephen's stoning is that he *stood* until the very last moment. Historically, when stoned, the accused was pushed off a platform into a shallow pit, then the accusers heaved stones down, usually striking the chest or head first, knocking the person down. Not so with Stephen. He stood the barrage until the end.

He refused to fall before these men. He didn't cower, but spoke to his God: "Receive my spirit." Only then did he fall to his *knees*, where he offered his last words, "Lord, do not hold this sin against them." True to the end, his fear and love of God was far greater and stronger than his fear of men. He didn't care what they did to him; he felt secure in his soon-to-be eternal home. Yet he still cared deeply about *their* need for approval from one another; enough to ask that their sins be forgiven.

A full-strength love for God means we have a greater fear and respect for the Lord than we do of any person. Our endurance and resolve lie in loving God more, much more, than wanting people's approval. "Whatever you do, work at it with all your heart, as working for the Lord, not for men, since you know that you will receive an inheritance from the Lord as a reward. It is the Lord Christ you are serving" (Colossians 3:23–24).

## DRAWING CLOSER TODAY

*Lord, I know in my heart you've created me with the ability to love and fear you more than my desire for any person's approval. Help me today to live out my higher love for you with all of my strength, standing firm on you as my rock.*

## TO KNOW HIM AS

# ALMIGHTY GOD

God is all mighty. He is mightier than all. Men may have killed Stephen and curtailed the flow of his words, but God was not defeated. His purpose was still accomplished. You can take a person out of this life, but you can't take the life of Christ out of a person.

When we know God as our Almighty Lord, we turn our backs on all else that we may know. With a circumcised heart and soul we can walk in the light of His wisdom, not fearing any human being, nor fearing death without hope of eternity in heaven.

Ours will be a godly death. A death that ushers our soul to heaven, yet will bring the knowledge of Christ to earth through our testimony that lives on.

*Who is "on center" in your life?*

Will you choose not to let the fear of people dilute your God-given wisdom? Instead, claim the Lord as your Almighty, your all in all, your be all and end all.

Memory Verse:

*He who dwells in the shelter of the Most High will rest in the shadow of the Almighty. I will say of the Lord, "He is my refuge and my fortress, my God, in whom I trust."*

*"Because he loves me," says the Lord, "I will rescue him; I will protect him, for he acknowledges my name. He will call upon me, and I will answer him; I will be with him in trouble, I will deliver him and honor him. With long life will I satisfy him and show him my salvation."*

PSALM 91:1–2, 14–16

# 6

# THE EARS OF A NATION:

*Loving Him in Unity*

TO KNOW HIM AS

*HOLY ONE*

READ: NEHEMIAH 8

# HEART

*All the people assembled as one man. . . .*

NEHEMIAH 8:1

The Israelites needed a cheerleader, and they found one in Nehemiah. He was a man who knew that the accomplishment of God's heart rested in the unity of the Israelite nation.

The book of Nehemiah tells us that the walls of Jerusalem were rebuilt in fifty-two days. Fifty-two *days*! The Israelites joined hands in their commitment to unity. Nehemiah 4:6 says, "So we rebuilt the wall till all of it reached half its height, for the people worked with all their heart." It takes a strong leader to keep people's hearts tender to the cause and eyes glued to the vision. Under the clear direction and watchful eyes of Nehemiah, disunity had no foothold in the project. When the walls were completed, the people returned to their villages with a spring in their step, confident in a job well done, and looked forward to gathering together again for the Feast of the Trumpets, the traditional festival of the civil new year.

With every ending is a new beginning, and this completion of the temple was the beginning of a new unified life for them. They spilled sweat together in the building, and now they wanted to be unified in understanding the why and for whom they had built the temple. So all the people gathered together "as one man in the square" (8:1), and they asked Ezra the scribe to read from the Book of the Law of Moses. There they "listened attentively" as he read the words of their forefathers' God (8:3).

Do we listen as attentively when God's Word is in the air? Are our collective hearts, like the restored Israelites, yearning to hear and understand God's Word? Do we have a deep desire to know what God's Word means for us personally and as a united church body (regardless of denomination)?

*He longs for us to have unity with Him, unity with individuals, and unity as a church—the bride of Christ.*

Nehemiah knew that God's preference and desire for us is unity of heart. He longs for us to have unity with Him, unity with individuals, and unity as a church—the bride of Christ. "How good and pleasant it is when brothers live together in unity! ... For there the Lord bestows his blessing, even life forevermore" (Psalm 133:1, 3).

When we love the Lord God with all our hearts, nothing

can stop us or deter us from seeking out His Word and what it means to us collectively. His words are life. They are what He wants us to know about who He is, His character, His faithfulness, His love, His forgiveness, and His like-mindedness for us. What is recorded in the Holy Bible is what God wants etched on our hearts. The details that God felt were important for us to understand are included, yet other details are not provided. Why? Not because the Lord wants to leave us with a half-finished jigsaw puzzle, but because He wants to draw our hearts closer to Him in unity. He gives us each a revealing piece that fits with and adds to His unified church.

DRAWING CLOSER TODAY

*Lord, thank you for your faithfulness in establishing communication with your people through your Word. I love your Word. I do desire to listen attentively to what the Holy Spirit will reveal to me and to the united body of Christ.*

# SOUL

*Ezra praised the Lord, the great God; and all the people lifted their hands and responded, "Amen! Amen!" Then they bowed down and worshiped the Lord with their faces to the ground.*

NEHEMIAH 8:6

I have stood with large groups of fellow Christians, from a couple hundred to thousands, as we've gathered for a conference or retreat. The praise and worship times act as a leveler. Denominations don't matter. Different skin colors blend into one. Worship styles comingle. In unity, the words and music drift up, gathering up our souls as the choruses reach heavenward. Love for the Lord comes from within as a result of the outward unified display. All that matters, the only care each person has is to worship the Lord from our saved-by-grace souls. We worship because we know what the Lord has done for us—and He deserves the praise.

Now, imagine being in the newly reunited group of forty-two thousand people in Nehemiah, chapter 8. That's a lot of people. I imagine they could make a lot of noise too. When Ezra opened the Book of the Law, the people stood up. What reverence and anticipation they expressed! When they lifted their hands, empty of all but praise, they showed they had brought nothing with them. This time of praise wasn't about communicating a need; it was about unity of worship.

When they praised, they looked heavenward. We often do the same thing. So why did they, and why do we, often bow heads for the reading of God's Word? It's partly to keep our eyes and souls from distraction as we listen to the Word of God, but even more, when we bow our heads, we move from corporate worship to personal vulnerability. We transition from collective unity to individual revelation. From the unity of collective worship, the doors to our souls swing open so the Lord can touch us with personal revelation. During these times He may show us how we have contributed to the disunity of His church.

The Israelites welcomed this revelation of their souls. They *wanted* it. The Lord had been exceedingly faithful in bringing them back from exile, to return them to a unified nation. Now they desired a similar restoration of their souls. They knew the integrity of their nation depended on the integrity of their individual souls.

Do we feel the same way? Do we truly, deeply, passionately understand that the integrity of the unity of Christ's church is dependent on our individual souls? Does this even matter to us? Do we too welcome the revelations in our soul of those thoughts, words, or actions that have prevented unity in Christ's church?

Loving the Lord with all of our soul means praying for and wanting revelation. We need to be willing to let the Lord reveal to us in what ways we might be loving Him with *less* of our soul. These aren't easy revelations; they are hard revelations. We may see that pride in our own church or judgment of other churches reveals a lesser soul-love for God.

*Do we truly, deeply, passionately understand that the integrity of the unity of Christ's church is dependent on our individual souls?*

God sent His only Son to die for *everyone*. He loves our souls equally. He doesn't love my neighbor's soul more than mine, nor does He love my soul more than yours. If we love Him with our whole soul, then doesn't it follow that we also love the souls of those He loves?

Can you take a lesson from the Israelites and welcome a revelation to your soul? It might even be a revelation about how you feel or act toward other people in His body. Christ didn't simply tolerate others' differences; He had no concern for different denominations. We invented that. To Him, we are all the same and are all worthy of being in holy union with Him, His bride—the church.

DRAWING CLOSER TODAY

*Lord, I desire to stand in heaven and worship you together with all your church. In that place I know there will be lasting unity and my soul-love for you will be complete. Even now, Lord, I pray for hard revelations in my spirit so that I may know a truer unity of your church.*

# MIND

*They read from the Book of the Law of God, making it clear and giving the meaning so that the people could understand what was being read.*

NEHEMIAH 8:8

Have you ever shed a tear of frustration over a lack of understanding about something? I have. From college courses to life circumstances, I've found myself in tears as my mind can't seem to get itself around a concept or understand a situation. "But I don't *get it*," I'll say, and stomp my feet impatiently.

I feel this way about God's Word sometimes. "Why, Lord?" I'll ask. Or, "I don't understand what this verse means!" I honestly do want to know God's mind about the verse I keep tripping over—even if the meaning suggests unpleasant consequences for me.

Such was the case for the Israelites when Ezra and the Levites read the Book of the Law. All their history—the reasons for the wars and tragedies, and the punishments and banishment—suddenly became clear to them. In our two earlier readings, we learned that they *wanted* to hear the Book of the Law. Their hearts and souls were ripe to hear. Like dried-out sponges, they thirsted to hear and understand the life-giving words.

Imagine for a moment how this felt to the Israelites. Just suppose that you had heard tidbits about how our nation came into being. But you weren't sure of the important characters and their stories, you couldn't name all the significant locations, and you hadn't heard much about the what or the why of the origin of our nation's laws. How confusing it would be to live in this country! There would be no unity of understanding about where we had come from, why we behave as we do, or where we are going. Bits and pieces of information might have dotted your understanding, but you desperately wanted to connect all the dots.

This is how the Israelites felt—they were desperate for information and understanding.

What was their response upon hearing and *finally* comprehending who they were and what God's plan was for them as a nation? They mourned. "For all the people had been weeping as they listened to the words of the Law" (8:9).

They *grieved*, because they now understood just how far their nation had strayed from their Lord. They cried for all the wasted years and the lost lives of their forefathers. They cried for themselves and for their children. They cried for things gone wrong that they couldn't change and the tragic consequences. They cried and wailed and grieved.

Oh, the relief in sudden divine understanding! "The unfolding of your words gives light" (Psalm 119:130). Just as the Israelites found, when we understand something from the Word of the Lord that has evaded us, we instantly find ourselves held captive to the new revelation. We were hostages before because we "didn't get it." Then, once we are free from confusion, we find ourselves captive again, this time to the new truth. But it's a safe captivity. It's safe because the Lord reveals something about His character when He answers our cry for understanding: He is faithful. His answer to our desire for understanding may even be "This is something you cannot know the earth-side of heaven, but trust me anyway." That's still an answer, and usually with this kind of answer comes the peace of knowing all is in His control.

*Once we are free from confusion, we find ourselves captive again, this time to the new truth.*

We have the assurance of eventual full understanding found in 1 Corinthians 13:12: "Then we shall see face to face. Now I know in part; then I shall know fully, even as I am fully known."

Loving the Lord with all our mind means being able to ask for revelation, then knowing the joy of understanding when it comes, or the peace of letting God hold it close to His heart until we reach His side. God created our minds to be ever seeking, ever learning, ever understanding. Loving Him whole-mindedly is an ongoing process, one in which we

will constantly gain a deeper understanding of who our great
God is.

DRAWING CLOSER TODAY
> *Lord, I'm grateful for the inquisitive mind you've given me.*
> *I thank you that I can ask you anything about your Word and*
> *you will be faithful to answer me in the way you deem best.*
> *I'll trust you to continually renew my mind according to your*
> *Word* (Romans 12:2).

# STRENGTH

*Do not grieve, for the joy of the Lord is
your strength.*

NEHEMIAH 8:10

The Father of Lies lives to destroy the body of Christ. Satan's top priority is to sap our strength and spiritual fervor, leaving us weak-kneed, immobile, and discouraged.

Such was the case when my husband and I, among other leaders in our church, found ourselves trying to stand up to the verbal blows from an angry, vindictive church member. We were shocked, felt betrayed, angry, and deeply hurt. We grieved the loss of relationships, brotherhood, and trust. Each feeling wormed its way into our hearts and minds until we felt hollow inside.

As these events unfolded, my husband, children, and I had an opportunity to visit family in another state. As we worshiped with them on Sunday morning, my spirit cried out for understanding. The pain and confusion about the situation at home was too much to bear, and the tears wouldn't stop slipping down my cheeks. But then, in the midst of worshiping with strangers, yet brothers and sisters in the Lord, a sweet joy began to fill my heart. As I lifted my hands to the Lord, His joy came down through my body and filled my empty soul. Where I had felt weakness, suddenly there was strength. Where I had felt deadened by confusion, there suddenly was a live understanding of God's heart in the situation. I felt His words impressed on my open heart, "Will you trust *me* in this?"

> *I felt His words impressed on my open heart, "Will you trust me in this?"*

My spirit answered, "Yes." Then, amazingly, I felt a deep compassion for the very person who was hurting our church and us so badly.

I wonder if this is how the Israelites felt when they wept and grieved over the sudden understanding of God's Book of the Law. Their grief was intense. Their sorrow profound. Their grief and sorrow weren't about betrayal, but about sudden understanding of things past. How did Ezra, Nehemiah, and the Levites respond to their tears? "Do not grieve, for the joy of the Lord is your strength."

It appears that the people may not have eaten before or while they gathered in the square to hear the Law read. Their bodies were empty. They came with nothing to eat; they just wanted God's Word as issued through the law written by

Moses to be their bread. They must have felt physically weak, standing packed together in an open square as the morning sun began to blaze down on their heads. They were crying; they must have started to feel thirsty. Nehemiah saw their physical need and released them to "Go and enjoy choice food and sweet drinks, and send some to those who have nothing prepared. This day is sacred to our Lord" (8:10).

Why was the day sacred? Because they no longer relied on their circumstances as a barometer of their feelings. They gained strength and joy because now they knew God in a more personal way. That was sacred to God. It was the accomplishment of His purpose in their lives, as it is in ours: to know Him better.

The joy of understanding God's heart renews our strength. We can't trust or depend on our own strength in any situation, especially a confusing one. Our strength is only found in the joy of knowing God's heart. The greater the joy that we are willing to receive from Him, the greater will be our strength to love Him and trust Him fully in any situation.

DRAWING CLOSER TODAY

*Lord, I'm willing to receive the joy only you can give me. I confess I'm feeling tired and hopeless about _____ . Forgive me for not trusting you for _____ . I receive the joy you have for me now, knowing the strength to worship and love you wholeheartedly will follow.*

TO KNOW HIM AS

# HOLY ONE

We share the one and only God. But being a jealous God, He won't share us. As His church, His bride, we are one, yet remarkably known and individual to Him.

We can collectively know Him by His Word. Just as the Israelites were thirsting for His Holy Word, we should too. The great truth is that He is true to His Word. Not the handshake-and-wink kind of human "true to one's word," but the *true-to-His-Word* kind of God, who is holy in all He does. That's what makes Him holy. He can't be *untrue* to His Word or to His people or to His unified church.

*Who is "on center" in your life?*

Can you, will you, wholeheartedly follow our one God, who will show himself holy and true to His Word?

Memory Verse:

*Exalt the Lord our God and worship at His footstool; he is holy. O Lord our God, you answered them; you were to Israel a forgiving God, though you punished their misdeeds. Exalt the Lord our God and worship at his holy mountain, for the Lord our God is holy.*

PSALM 99:5, 8–9

# 7

# A LIGHT IN THE DARK:

*Loving Him With Confidence*

TO KNOW HIM AS

## MOST HIGH

READ: PROVERBS 31

# HEART

*Her husband has full confidence in her. . . .*
*She provides food for her family and*
*portions for her servant girls. . . . She opens*
*her arms to the poor and extends her hands*
*to the needy.*

PROVERBS 31:11, 15, 20

My high school occasionally relaxed the dress code for "dress-down day," "backward day," or my favorite, "inside-out day." The inside-out day showed us to be poor menders with white, holey pockets flapping, thready seams showing, and tags hanging.

Now as an adult, I see a much humbler side—a spiritual application—to walking through one's day "inside out." Just as inside-out clothes can't hide holes and unraveling thread, neither can we completely hide what's inside our heart from the outside world.

The Proverbs 31 woman is an inside-out person. She defines a woman who sees the fullness of life beyond herself! She has a heart of tender compassion for other people in her life, particularly her family. Her heart isn't heavy with her own concerns, but light with kindness for those people whom the Lord has made important to her. She wears the convictions of her inner heart on the outside of her life through her actions.

We can reflect our love for the Lord through an extension to the outside of what's inside. The Proverbs 31 woman has so much love for her Lord that she "extends her hands to the needy."

But what if what's inside isn't full-heart love for the Lord? What if something else resides in our heart where God-love should be? I know that one of the biggest disgraces of my heart is self-importance.

We entertain the sin of self-importance when we elevate our situations, our positions, our thoughts, or ourselves as superior to others. We all have the natural edge of competitiveness. Maybe it's inborn—"survival of the fittest." But that competitiveness becomes sin when we vainly believe that our personhood is *more important* than someone else's. It's personal confidence gone awry.

Self-importance shows its ugly head when we feel we need to be the center of attention. Or when we need others not only to *hear* what we have to say but also to *agree* with what we say. It can be a need to be needed or a need to be valued. Self-importance is when we have to get a word in about our success or accomplishments.

Self-importance is to have built a throne in our heart, where we sit comfortably in the spotlight. That's idolatry. And if we're on the throne in our heart, where's the Lord—the one who is supposed to be in the center of our heart and whom we are supposed to love with all of our being?

*If we're on the throne in our heart, where's the Lord?*

If we've wrapped our arms around ourselves, we can't "open [our] arms to the poor and extend [our] hands to the needy." If *we* are on the inside, *we* are going to show on the outside. If we are on the throne of love in our heart, instead of the Lord, we can't minister in His name—we're ministering in our own name. Actually, we aren't ministering at all. Do you know how far that kind of "love" will extend? About two inches.

Humility needs to replace self-importance. That's why self-importance is a disgrace to our hearts. We've egotistically sat in the place of grace that is reserved for the Lord.

The Lord is exceedingly patient, however. He won't force His way past our ego. He always offers us a choice. If we choose to love Him with all our heart, we must remove our self from the center of our heart. When He's on the inside, and our heart is submitted to Him, that's what will show on the outside.

DRAWING CLOSER TODAY

*Lord, let my life be all about you. I confess those areas where self-importance has dominated my heart's throne. Today help me to return the throne of grace to you, so that I will be inside out, and only you will be showing on the outside.*

# SOUL

*Her lamp does not go out at night.*

PROVERBS 31:18

This is a verse I once struggled with. I prayed, *Lord, I know this confident woman is someone I need to aspire to. She has many qualities I can relate to: she's a businesswoman, she's supportive of her husband's work, she tends her house well, and her children respect her.*

*But, Lord, her lamp doesn't go out at night. She stays up all night? I'm not sure I can be this woman. Heavenly Father, you created me, and you know I need lots of sleep. I can't not sleep!*

He gently corrected me. The Proverbs 31 woman sleeps plenty: consider the reference to her bed in verse 15, "She gets up while it is still dark," and to her sleeping comfort in verse 22, "She makes coverings for her bed." Plus, she wouldn't have the energy for her multitasking if she didn't sleep.

The reference to her all-night-burning lamp is really two-fold.

First, it tells us that she's prepared. Her lamp doesn't go out, because she's filled it with the fuel it needs to keep burning. She has anticipated how much oil she'll need, she takes the time to fill the lamp, and she trims the wick so as not to waste any fuel.

Second, and I'd say more important, the inextinguishable lamp represents her inner lamp—the fire in her soul. What is that fire? The Spirit of the living God. We have that same lamp in us. "You are my lamp, O Lord" (2 Samuel 22:29).

*When the night watch seems unbearably long and dark, it is the very time when we most need to love the Lord enough to keep stubbornly dipping into the fuel of His Word.*

In every person's life, there will inevitably come times of darkness. These night watches are when our soul feels dark with confusion or hurt or depression or defeat. You've experienced them, and so have I. Our soul may feel abandoned and lost. But we need to keep watch; we need to keep our inner lamp burning, even if it is dim and sputtering with the last drops of fuel.

This is when our soul-love for the Lord rekindles the threatened flame. Our love for God and His Word is the fuel. When the night watch seems unbearably long and dark, it is the very time when we most need to love the Lord enough to keep stubbornly dipping into the fuel of His Word.

The Proverbs 31 woman's lamp does not go out at night,

because when she's faced with discouragement, she knows she has prepared her inner lamp with the fuel from God's Word. The second part of 2 Samuel 22:29 reads: "The Lord turns my darkness into light." God's love for us will turn our defeated, sputtering lamps into a renewed full flame.

However, the fuel of His Word can only feed our inner lamp when we have filled our soul with it. It's our responsibility. A full-fledged soul-love for the Lord requires daily preparation for times of darkness. His promise is certain: His light will be inextinguishable in you when your spirit is full of His fuel.

### DRAWING CLOSER TODAY

*Lord, I want to commit to filling my soul every day with your Word. I know this commitment is a reflection of my full love for you. And I'll trust that when dark times come, this fuel I've stored up will light my path.*

# MIND

*She speaks with wisdom, and faithful
instruction is on her tongue.*

PROVERBS 31:26

For three years I home-educated one or both of my children. It was simultaneously a deep heart-call and a frightening responsibility—not something I took lightly. One of my objectives as teacher to my children was to be a consistent instructor: consistent in my nurture, discipline, love, and expectations. I knew my children would suffer in their education if I didn't respect their need for structure and consistency.

When I read the words above about the Proverbs 31 mother speaking with "faithful instruction," I think about how our love for the Lord is reflected in the words we say to our children. Are our words faithful to how much we love, honor, and respect our heavenly Father? Do we talk about

Him with consistency? Is His Word, memorized Scripture, quick on our tongues to offer comfort, correction, and love? I want to be confident and faithful with the instruction He has entrusted to me to pass on to my children. I'd guess you do too.

The first part of this verse offers even more definition of how and what we are to say. It reminds us that first come the thoughts in our minds, hopefully wise thoughts, and then come the words from our mouths.

Have you ever had a conversation with someone who talks impulsively? He doesn't think; he just speaks. I can have a lashing tongue; the Lord constantly reminds me that I need to have better control of it. With all the people whose feelings I've hurt, including my family, I can understand why James wrote with such conviction about the tongue

> *Once a dam is broken, you can't reroute the water back to its source. So it is with our words.*

starting a fire (3:6). Too many times I've wished I could quickly catch those words midair and stuff them back in my mouth. It's the five-seconds-too-late phenomenon. Once a dam is broken, you can't reroute the water back to its source. So it is with our words.

When we hurt people with our words, who feels the pain the most? I believe it hurts and grieves our Lord. Why? Because He loves the person we've hurt, and He loves us, and He hates to see strife between us. That's why Christ said the second greatest commandment, to love our neighbor, is like the first. Both are based on love. Paul says in Romans 15:5–6, "[May God] give you the spirit of unity among yourselves as you follow Christ Jesus, so that with one heart and mouth you may glorify the God and Father of our Lord Jesus Christ."

When we love the Lord with all our mind, it means we have His wisdom in store. How do we store up His wisdom? We collect wisdom by loving to fill our minds with His Word, because it's His *words*.

Have you ever received a love letter? You reread the words over and over until they were deep in your mind, and your heart *knew* every nuance. So it should be with how we love the Lord and His Word. There's a domino effect: The more we study His Word, the more we love it. The more we love it, the more God's wisdom grows in our minds. The more our minds understand wise thoughts, the more we'll speak with wisdom.

Speaking with wisdom born of a mind-love for God and His Holy Word means we apply His Word appropriately—at the right time, at the right place, with the right words, to the right people. Our spiritual confidence builds with each correctly handled situation.

DRAWING CLOSER TODAY

*Lord, I desire my words to be full of your wisdom. I love your Word. I treasure it. Convict me of those times when I've spoken in a manner that may have grieved you. Please forgive me. Replace my words with yours.*

# STRENGTH

*She considers a field and buys it; out of her earnings she plants a vineyard. She sets about her work vigorously; her arms are strong for her tasks.*

PROVERBS 31:16–17

The Proverbs 31 woman is a highly gifted woman. Not only is she a wife, mother, and employer, she's a real estate investor and businesswoman. She's a respected leader in her community. She also shows artistry in a number of creative projects.

I like this woman! She's the kind of friend who has lots of friends. Either intentionally or unintentionally, she's mentoring younger women around her, even her own daughters. I envision her as a mature woman, not necessarily in years, but in her faith. She knows from where she draws her spiritual strength and energy. She knows what motivates her. She has learned that when her heart is God-directed, her actions have a heavenly impact. Her life statement might be "I know my Creator is watching me to see how I will use what He has entrusted to me. I want to be worthy of His trust."

What a high calling! We sometimes forget what a privilege it is to be God's workers, *entrusted* by an all-powerful God to do His work. I consider that a tremendous honor.

With what does He entrust us? Many things, including our gifts and skills. The strength-love we have for the Lord shows in the recognition of our gifts and the effective use of them. Our divine gifts are what God has equipped us with and entrusted to us as "strength" for His purposes.

This understanding of gifting draws to mind the parable of the talents as told in Matthew 25:14–30. We know the story well: the frightened man who buried his talent was chastened and exiled by the employer. The zealous businessman who doubled his share found a place of honor with his employer and was entrusted with even more responsibility.

All three of the key players recognized who owned the talents in the first place. They never had ownership. Their master always did. Paralleled to us, the master is our Lord. He has lent us the gifts that He wants us to use and multiply. They are on loan. We are entrusted with them.

The Proverbs 31 woman not only knows what her gifts and strengths are, she is *confident* enough in them to "spend" them, knowing they will be replenished above and beyond what is being offered. The more she uses her gifts, the more there will be to use again.

We have some exceedingly wealthy friends. Philanthropists at heart, they gladly give away their money to noble causes, research, and nonprofit organizations. Their goal is to give it all away, yet they know they can never spend it all. The interest alone overrides their giving.

Though I'm hesitant to draw a parallel between spending money and the Lord, there exists a similarity. Our undivided love for God calls us to use what He's given us with vigor and without hesitation. Our full-strength love for Him is reflected in how much we are willing to "spend" our gifts. Loving God with all of our strength means we continuously try to "spend" our gifts in full. Not because we want to get rid of them, but because there's always a ready supply.

That's why our Proverbs 31 woman can "laugh at the days to come" (v. 25). She's not worried about her gifts being depleted. She knows her strength in the Lord can never be exhausted. She looks forward to the days ahead as she demonstrates her love for Him by using the gifts and skills He's given her.

*It seems that if we spend our gifts we'll feel weak and depleted. But God isn't a taker. He's a giver.*

It seems that if we spend our gifts we'll feel weak and depleted. But God isn't a taker. He's a giver. He'll replenish what we've been faithful to spend. He promises to make up the difference: "Give, and it will be given to you" (Luke 6:38).

## DRAWING CLOSER TODAY

*Lord, I thank you for the divine gifts you've given me. Show me where I've been miserly and not willing to spend what you've entrusted to me. I pray for a fuller strength-love for you so I can "spend" the gifts you've given me. I'll trust you to replenish them.*

TO KNOW HIM AS

# MOST HIGH

When I was a child, I thought there surely had to be an end to the heavens. I envisioned a brick wall or some sort of barrier in the sky that kept the earth and the planets and the stars inside. Even now, as an adult, it's impossible for me to fathom infinity. Everything we know and are exposed to all our lives is finite. It all has an end point.

Except our Lord. There is no end to Him; there is no end to the heavens He created. Where He dwells is the most high place, because He is Most High. There is nothing higher; there is nothing fathomable about the extent of His reign. Just as our eyes can't see an end to the heavens, our minds won't know a limit to God. What He does want us to know is that He is limitless.

Our confidence in God being God rests in knowing there is no other above or beside Him. The Proverbs 31 woman knew in her confidence and faithfulness that the purpose was to serve not just those around her, but the Most High. Like her, the calling on our lives is higher than the horizon of our eyesight.

Who is "on center" in your life?

In confidence, will you look beyond that which you can
see, and know that the Lord is Most High in the world
and in your life?

Memory Verse:
*My shield is God Most High, who saves the upright in heart.*

PSALM 7:10

# 8

# THE BREAD OF
# ADVERSITY:

*Loving Him With Thanksgiving*

TO KNOW HIM AS

## HEALER

READ: LUKE 17:11–19

# HEART

*As [Jesus] was going into a village, ten men*
*who had leprosy met him. They stood at a*
*distance and called out in a loud voice,*
*"Jesus, Master, have pity on us!"*

LUKE 17:12–13

It's been said that misery loves company. In the case of
the lepers, they probably didn't *love* the fact that by
law they were forced to live together, but at least in
their misery they had company. Their mutual adversity of disease linked them as a codependent group, but separated them from their homes and families.

How desperate they must have felt to reconnect with
healthy people! How they must have yearned for freedom
from their forced mutual dependency. As Jesus walked nearby,
one can imagine them wistfully looking on, hoping to catch
His eye. They knew who He was; they knew He could make

them well. They knew through Him they could be welcomed back into their old lives.

The lepers also knew they could not approach Christ. They had a potentially contagious disease. It was an ugly disease, their flesh raw and oozing—too disgusting to look at, too dangerous to get close to.

Because of this flesh disease, they were separated from Christ. The condition of their flesh ruled their lives. Hmmm. Aren't we too, because of our "flesh," separated from Christ? Romans 3:23 says, "For all have sinned and fall short of the glory of God," and Romans 6:23, "For the wages of sin is death." There's a price to pay for sin, and the cost is death in all its forms: spiritual death, broken relationships, and lost hopes. While in sin, we find ourselves, like the lepers, disconnected, lonely, and separated from the fullness of community only found in the Lord's family.

When the lepers called Jesus "Master," what they were really saying was *"We want you to be Master over our flesh. We want healing for our flesh and, even more, we want to be linked to you as Master. We don't want to be separated any longer."*

*Because of this flesh disease, they were separated from Christ. The condition of their flesh ruled their lives.*

I think all ten lepers believed this with all their heart. They had good, honest intentions. Yet, only one returned with a heart of true gratitude and worship for the One who had healed him. He now could return to his home, his family (if he had one), and his former life. You can imagine he danced and skipped and jumped all the way home, so full of love and joy and praise for his healing. He had a story to tell!

At the end of this thankful-leper story, the healed man is facedown in the dirt at Christ's feet. I can imagine the Lord reaching out His hand to touch the man's shoulder as He said, "Rise up and go." Jesus touched more than his shoulder. He touched his heart. The Lord touched it in such a profound and intimate way that the man now knew who his Master would be for the rest of his life. And that master wasn't his "flesh" disease any longer.

When we love the Lord with all our heart, He is our forever Master. Our flesh—our tendency to sin—can no longer rule over us. Not that we'll stop sinning; that's a lifetime condition. But sin can no longer hold mastery over us or limit us from kneeling at Christ's feet and asking Him to touch our carnal nature and change it.

"For sin shall not be your master, because you are not under law, but under grace.... But now that you have been set free from sin and have become slaves to God, the benefit you reap leads to holiness, and the result is eternal life" (Romans 6:14, 22).

## Drawing Closer Today

*Lord, I pray that I will have a heart committed to following you solely as my forever Master. Thank you for welcoming me into your family, and that I never again need to look on from a distance. I want to be focused entirely on you, not turning to my right or to my left (Deuteronomy 5:32).*

# SOUL

*He threw himself at Jesus' feet and thanked
him—and he was a Samaritan.
"Was no one found to return and give
praise to God except this foreigner?"*

LUKE 17:16, 18

**M**y father is a carpenter. As a child I spent
countless hours in his workshop, watching his
calloused, strong hands fashion rough-hewn
pine and cherry boards into Shaker reproduc-
tions. Sometimes I'd play with my father's leftover pieces of
wood, nailing or gluing the cast-off bits to create doll furni-
ture or miniature houses.

I imagine young Jesus may have done the same thing in
Joseph's carpenter shop. Eying his father's strong hands,
maybe He too experimented with the discarded pieces, not
letting any go to waste.

The training ground of His father's workshop prepared

Jesus to live out one of the principles of His ministry: there is no waste in God's economy. All pieces are usable; nothing is ever too small or broken or ugly. In his father's shop He learned that He could fashion something beautiful from bits of nothing.

*In his father's shop He learned that He could fashion something beautiful from bits of nothing.*

This lesson came in handy when Jesus found himself facing the brokenness and ugliness of the lepers. Twice Luke points out that the thankful leper belonged to the "foreign" Samaritan sect. Not only was the leper an outsider due to his faith but he was also an outcast due to his ugly disease. This was a double flaw to which the disciples wanted to give a wide berth.

But, of course, Jesus didn't see the lepers that way. He saw something of worth. He saw their brokenness, but instead of only looking at the jagged, splintered edges, He saw value. As with the cast-off wood in His father's workshop, He saw their potential and said, "I can use those broken people. I can create something new out of them."

He not only healed the tenth leper's outer wounds, but He also healed His inner hurt. Jesus took the pain of being cast off and created a complete, whole new person.

So what happened to the remaining nine lepers who also found their bodies transformed by Christ's healing words? Their silence of ingratitude is just one of the many betrayals of Christ before His final betrayal on the cross. They discarded any thought of thankfulness as they ran to the priest for confirmation. Even in their healing they betrayed their Healer. Why didn't they say thank you? Because their souls were not affected by the healing. Their healing was only skin deep, stopping short of their souls. Only the one who returned in gratitude had let the healing sink deep into his soul. Out of his brokenness, his soul was restored.

Jesus can and will use the adversity in our lives that causes feelings of brokenness and hopelessness. Adversity is not wasted. It is useful to build something new. He used the unlovable, the sick, and the outsiders to show His mastery.

It takes a carpenter's eye to see the potential in a rough, stained piece of wood. Christ's vision for us is no less than what He did for the leper. He sees our broken pieces. He picks up the cast-off bits of our lives. He says, "I can use these." Then He gently rebuilds them into something beautiful that will reflect His craftsmanship.

DRAWING CLOSER TODAY

*Lord, thank you that you make use of everything in my life—even those things that I see as beyond hope. I pray that I will always be thankful for whatever pieces you are refashioning in my life.*

# MIND

*When he saw them, he said, "Go, show yourselves to the priests." And as they went, they were cleansed.*

LUKE 17:14

What did Jesus do when He looked at the lepers standing at a distance and calling to Him? The above Scripture says He "saw" them. He saw their ailments, He saw them waving their arms at Him, and He saw the emotional pain etched on their faces. He heard their pleading voices and the desperation in their words. His senses were touched by their outward appearance; His compassion was pricked by their deeper cry for healing.

Our senses are processed in our brain. Unconsciously, our minds filter information through our senses. The nine lepers who walked away *heard* Christ's words of healing and *saw* it to be true as they dashed to the priest for confirmation. The tenth leper, who gave thanks, took his healing one step further, or rather, closer to Christ. He heard and saw, just as the first nine did, but then the healing traveled past the external—his mind filtering his senses—and reached into his heart. His mind *received* internal healing as well as physical healing.

This brings to mind Christ's parable of the sower found earlier in Luke 8:4–15. Jesus tells the story of the sower spreading the seed, and He ends the account with a challenge: "He who has ears to hear, let him hear" (8:8). With these words He confirmed that not everyone has the ears to hear God's Word, nor the heart to receive it. The disciples immediately asked, "What does this parable mean?"

Christ's explanation sheds a lot of light on humanity. First, I believe He means that the entire world will have the opportunity to hear the Word of God, but that "the devil [will come] and take away the Word from their hearts." Second, the people with hardened hearts will not be able to receive the Word, because there's no place for it to take root. The third group receives the Word of God, and they grow a little, but then they die from the distractions of life. And the last group, where you and I want to be, stands for the people who *hear, receive*, and then *hold on to* what they know to be true. "But the seed on good soil stands for those with a noble and good heart, who hear the word, retain it, and by persevering produce a crop" (Luke 8:15).

"Good soil" has the sound of expectancy, doesn't it? It anticipates growing useful crops. In the fertile land of our minds we want the Lord to plant knowledge. We want Him to grow seedlings of wisdom in our hearts. We know when we come into a love relationship with Him, that we can expect and anticipate the revelation of His Word in us.

*We hold the Word in trust for future needs in our lives.*

Good soil also *retains* God's Word. In legal terms, a retainer is a deposit given to hold against future expenses and expenditures. I like how that fits with our Christian perspective of retaining the Holy Word. We hold the Word in trust for future needs in our lives.

What did the tenth leper "hold in trust?" He held a heart of love and thanksgiving for what the Lord had done for him. He retained the Lord's words of healing, and he held them in trust, expectantly anticipating how his healing would glorify God. It would bring glory not only in his life but also in the lives of others.

I too want to hold in trust those truths that the Lord has revealed to me. I love that He's trusted me with them.

He gives us nuggets of His truth that we hold not self-ishly, but securely in outstretched hands, anticipating how and when those truths can be used for His glory. Like the tenth leper, we can have thankful hearts and minds overjoyed with love at what the Lord has entrusted to us: His healing Word.

DRAWING CLOSER TODAY

*Heavenly Father, thank you for the ways you heal me. Ways I'm not always aware of. Thank you that you don't want to leave me broken. Thank you that healing comes from your Word. I will hold in trust those words of healing, for now and for the future.*

# STRENGTH

*Then he said to him, "Rise up and go; your faith has made you well."*

LUKE 17:19

In my wallet I carry a major credit card. I use it mostly for business expenses, and I pay the full balance each month. The card company tells me I have good credit, and they suggest I'm a good "risk" because I'm faithful in my payments. My credit is good because I'm a credible patron. I've earned the status of being dependable.

I want that same kind of dependable credibility with God. Not that I can earn it; God's love is freely given and must be freely received. But I do want to be counted as a trustworthy partner with my Lord. I want to be a credible witness to who He is and what He has done for me.

The tenth leper stood as a credible witness. His credit history was his healed leprosy: he was sick, and then he was well.

When Christ said to the leper, "Rise up and go," He was telling him to stand up. It may have been a few short words, but they are deep with meaning: *Stand up in the adversity. Stand up in the lessons you've just learned. Take strength in your new knowledge and GO! Go talk about it. Go tell people your story. Go witness about what I have done in your life. You are a credible person to speak of such things because you have suffered much.*

Isaiah 30:20 says, "Although the Lord gives you the bread of adversity and the water of affliction, your teachers will be hidden no more; with your own eyes you will see them." The teachers spoken of are Christ and His Word. And what do they teach? *Through* the adversity and affliction, there is something to learn—something of profit to take away. There is always a lesson to learn from the Lord through the process of affliction.

I believe that the tenth leper realized this and felt sudden profound thankfulness that he had been given the "bread of adversity" so he would be credible in his testimony of Christ.

I love hearing other people's testimonies. Yet there were times when I felt a tad jealous of others' profound conversion stories. My testimony sounded trivial by comparison: I was born and raised in a Christian home. I accepted Christ as my Savior at five, committed my life to Him at thirteen, and married a godly man at twenty. Not much excitement there. The more thrilling other people's stories were, the more I thought mine was boring.

But then the Lord gave me a taste of the "bread of adversity." It was bitter. It was hard to swallow. Once I internalized all the lessons He needed to teach me through that time in my life, I knew I had a story to tell, a message of victory. The adversity was my teacher.

When the Lord gives us adversity, He's proving that He loves us enough to want us to learn something about His character through the hardship. Through adversity is revelation, and in that revelation, strength.

A number of years ago our high altitude town experienced one of the worst ice storms in history, downing trees like matchsticks. Birch trees, being a "softer" wood, bent nearly in half, the top branches dragging on the ground. Weeks later, after the ice melted and the birches had begun to spring back to their full height, I learned that birches respond to the terrible stress of bending by laying down added tough fibers at the point of the bend. The reinforced trunk and branches are witness to the bending experience, but they are stronger than ever thereafter.

*When the Lord gives us adversity, He's proving that He loves us enough to want us to learn something about His character through the hardship.*

In Ephesians, Paul urges his fellow workers to "live a life worthy of the calling" (4:1). In adversity, let's be credible witnesses, desiring to be worthy of what the Lord has called us to be and to do. Let's trust Him to give us added strength when the adversity bends us to breaking, always holding on to the promise that "a bruised reed he will not break" (Isaiah 42:3).

DRAWING CLOSER TODAY

*I thank you, Lord, for the bending process. I thank you that you do count me worthy of adversity, so that I can be a witness of your character and sustaining love.*

TO KNOW HIM AS

# HEALER

The healed lepers learned that our Lord is an up-close-and-personal God. Healing doesn't come from Christ when we are at a distance. It comes when we get close to Him. And He's not interested in just one kind of healing. He's a multifaceted Healer—purposing to heal our interior being as well as our exterior: body, mind, and soul.

Isaiah said it best when he prophesied about the coming of Christ, the Healer: "Surely he took up our infirmities and carried our sorrows. . . . But he was pierced for our transgressions, he was crushed for our iniquities; the punishment that brought us peace was upon him, and by his wounds we are healed" (53:4–5).

*Who is "on center" in your life?*

Even in the midst of difficulties, will you faithfully keep Christ at the center of your discomfort, knowing His presence is where the healing and comfort lie?

Memory Verse:
*He said, "If you listen carefully to the voice of the Lord your God and do what is right in his eyes, if you pay attention to his commands and keep all his decrees, I will not bring on you any of the diseases I brought on the Egyptians, for I am the Lord, who heals you."*

EXODUS 15:26

# 9

# A PLATE OF ENCOURAGEMENT:

## *Loving Him in Serving*

TO KNOW HIM AS

## *FRIEND*

READ: LUKE 10:38–42

# HEART

*[Jesus] came to a village where a woman
named Martha opened her home to him.*

LUKE 10:38

The state of our home really says what's important to us, doesn't it? It's been said that you can read the heart of a home by what's sitting on the coffee table. The temper of our hearts is reflected by what reading material accumulates there.

It's obvious in the story of Martha and Mary that Martha had the gift of hospitality. She loved to entertain; she loved to invite people in and serve them. She wasn't too worried about her coffee table—it was free from clutter and dust.

Martha so often gets the short end of the stick in this story of hospitality. We're too quick to judge her "busyness." There's much more to Martha than her flurry of activity. There's a deeper meaning at work here, behind the initial comparison of the two ways the sisters interacted with the Lord.

When Martha "opened her home" to her Lord and Savior, she willingly opened her *heart* for His examination. Talk about being vulnerable! She welcomed her heart's inspection by the one who knew her heart better then anyone.

She knew what He'd find in her home and her heart: A genuine love for her friend. With such love she wanted to do what she did best: serve Him with unbridled devotion.

What would we do in similar circumstances? Instead of asking WWJD, ask yourself WWID (What Would I Do?). Do we have things in our heart, the home of who we are, that we think we need to clean up before we can welcome Christ to come in and take a look around? Or do we willingly allow Him access, knowing we need to clean up a bit, but that He'll help us with the task?

*As we welcome Christ into our heart-home, we want to do so motivated by love, not obligation. He'll never be a demanding visitor.*

As we welcome Christ into our heart-home, we want to do so motivated by love, not obligation. He'll never be a demanding visitor. He'll never point a finger and turn away in disgust at the disgraceful dust bunnies under the freezers of our lives. Why not? Because He knows our hearts' intent. We need to be openly vulnerable about who we are with Him. He knows us anyway, but He wants us to be willing to welcome

Him in and share the "dirt" with Him.

There is comfort in knowing we don't have to offer any pretenses about our heart-homes. We are just called to love Him without hesitation, without restrictions, to different rooms in our hearts, and with a welcoming attitude. First John says it all: "This then is how we know that we belong to the truth, and how we set our hearts at rest in his presence whenever our hearts condemn us. For God is greater than our hearts, and he knows everything" (3:19–20).

## DRAWING CLOSER TODAY

*Lord, I desire to welcome you into my heart, its unclean areas and all. I know that's what true love for you is: an open door to my heart and life.*

# SOUL

*[Martha] had a sister called Mary, who sat
at the Lord's feet listening to what he
said. . . . [Martha] asked, "Lord, don't you
care that my sister has left me to do the
work by myself? Tell her to help me!"*

LUKE 10:39–40

A teacher at heart, my daughter tries to instruct her younger brother on how to do things the right way—*her* way—and finds herself frustrated when he responds as an unwilling student. She jumps between policing him and mothering him, and he doesn't want any part of it.

In Martha and Mary's family, Martha must have been the older sister, as she has a distinct older sibling predisposition: bossy and self-righteous. In a way, we all act like older siblings. We think we've got the only answer, the only right way of doing things.

A Heart After God

Such was Martha's state of mind. We see two extremes between Mary and Martha in the story. Mary is sitting still; Martha is on the move. Mary is listening; Martha wants to be listened to. Mary is being fed; Martha wants to feed others. And where are their respective souls in this exchange at the Lord's feet? Mary has a soul filled with peace, and Martha has a soul full of self-righteousness.

Where did Martha go wrong? She started with good intentions: a heart to serve. So what happened? She allowed judgment of Mary's inactivity to influence her own actions. Then, remarkably, she tried to drag Jesus into it! She asked Him to make Mary feel *guilty* for not helping. She was right on only one count: Christ *could* have issued words of conviction that would have touched Mary's soul into activity. He could have, but He didn't. Why?

Because she was free from guilt. She was silent and still and listening—all without guilt.

That's hard for us to grasp in our "do more" culture, isn't it? We've perpetuated the lie that we will find success and be happier and more fulfilled if we just *do more*. Admit it, don't you feel just a little guilty if you do *nothing* for a day? No neat check marks next to your "to do" list, no accomplishments to relay to your family. Nothing to show for your day. What would that kind of day amount to? A sense of guilt.

But what if the day was used to simply spend time in God's Word—a day of fasting from everything else, all other responsibilities. Would you feel guilty then? Hopefully not.

Yet that's what the argument between Mary and Martha

158

was about: Martha tried to place guilt on Mary for doing something different than what Martha was doing. Can't you see Martha tapping her foot impatiently before the Lord? "It's Mary's fault that I feel so pressured. She should be helping!"

I love Mary's response. She said nothing. Why not? For two reasons: first, because she knew her soul didn't need to feel guilty. Maybe she was thinking, *When can time spent with the Lord ever be time ill-spent?* Second, she entrusted the Lord to answer for her. He knew her reasons for sitting quietly with Him. She didn't need to justify anything—even to her own sister.

Our deepening soul-love for the Lord teaches us how to discern between man-imposed guilt and true Holy-Spirit-justified guilt. How can we tell man-imposed guilt from the Holy Spirit's conviction? Take a cue from Mary: listen to Christ's words, and let Him speak for us. What Martha intended as convicting words toward Mary, Christ took and gently turned into a rebuke back to Martha. What did He say to Martha? "Mary has chosen what is better, and it will not be taken away from her" (Luke 10:42). He was saying, "Don't even think about trying to make her feel guilty for doing the right thing: listening to me."

*When can time spent with the Lord ever be time ill-spent?*

In Christ we are free to allow Him to convict us when necessary and equally free from false blame and accusation from others. Our soul-love for Christ can trust Him to distinguish the two for us.

DRAWING CLOSER TODAY

*Thank you, Lord Jesus, that you are the only one I need to answer to. I will trust you to convict me when necessary. I will also trust that my growing soul-love for you will teach me to let you speak on my behalf when necessary.*

# MIND

*Mary . . . sat at the Lord's feet listening to
what he said.*
*"Only one thing is needed. Mary has
chosen what is better, and it will not be
taken away from her."*

LUKE 10:39, 42

Wouldn't you like to know just what it was
that Christ spoke about as Mary sat enrap-
tured at His feet? We can speculate about a
number of things He may have been teach-
ing at their house. Maybe He pointed out a life application
lesson that was taking place at that moment: Gain a heart and
mind of wisdom by listening to His words. Maybe He also
reflected on the critical life lesson He had recently confirmed
with the Pharisees (vv. 25–29), and the premise for our entire
lives: Love all of Him with all of our being, and show loving-
kindness to our neighbors (vv. 30–37).

I suspect He talked about each of these things at Mary and Martha's house. This was the secret to the Christian faith, this was the answer to all their questions: Love the Lord God with all your heart, soul, mind, and strength. Of course, Mary listened wholeheartedly.

Mary desired to be taught. She knew her own mind was limited in her knowledge and understanding of Christ's teachings. Perhaps she even had an inkling that she wouldn't have many more chances to be with the Lord, and she wanted to treasure every word—food preparation with Martha took a distant second place.

A conscious choice took place in Mary's mind: fix food versus listen to her Lord. Hmmm. Pretty much a no-brainer, wouldn't you say? The Lord confirmed Mary's choice by saying to a ruffled Martha, "Only one thing is needed." What one thing? Listening to what the Lord was saying.

When Mary listened with all of her mind, she was inviting the Lord to show her any wrong in her life. It really was very similar to Martha's opening her home to him. In both cases the women were willing and openly vulnerable to letting the Lord *in*: into their home and into their heart, mind, and soul.

When Mary welcomed the Lord's words into her mind, she was asking to be taught. She wanted to know how and in what ways she needed to change to be able to love and worship her Savior more. She may have been silently praying, *Change my mind, Lord.*

That's a hard prayer to get past our lips, isn't it? *Change my mind, Lord.* Not change someone else (much too easy to pray that prayer). Not change the situation. But change *me. Change the way I see things. Change the way I understand things. Show me where I'm wrong. Give me your mind instead.*

Mary was anticipating that the Lord would indeed change her mind and give her renewed understanding about who He was. How do we know this? Because she doesn't speak throughout the whole exchange. She is speechless as Christ's words change her mind, her heart, and her soul. He was doing a profound work in her, even as she sat there! I suspect she didn't want to speak until He was finished with His work.

I don't like change. I don't welcome it. I can be a stubborn stick-to-the-way-I've-always-done-it person. Few of us like, anticipate, or welcome changes that will diminish our own self-important way of thinking. But when we love the Lord with all our mind, we need to welcome those new understandings that reveal more of Him. Paul reminds us why we should desire that the Lord change our minds: "Do not conform any longer to the pattern of this world, but be transformed by the renewing of your mind" (Romans 12:2).

> *That's a hard prayer to get past our lips, isn't it? Change my mind, Lord.*

DRAWING CLOSER TODAY

*Lord, I want to welcome a transformation of my mind. I love you with all my mind, and I ask you to daily change my mind to your mind.*

# STRENGTH

*As Jesus and his disciples were on their way,*
*he came to a village where a woman named*
*Martha opened her home to him. . . .*
*Martha was distracted by all the*
*preparations that had to be made. She came*
*to him and asked, "Lord, don't you care that*
*my sister has left me to do the work by*
*myself? Tell her to help me!"*

LUKE 10:38, 40

Wash the dishes, cook the food, sweep the house—busy, busy, busy. Not much has changed since Martha's day. I can see her standing at the door, greeting friends, taking cloaks, and directing traffic. She was a take-charge woman who expected others to follow.

Poor Martha, she lived ahead of her time. Just like women today, she led a multitasking life as a multi-gifted woman.

Not only did she have the gift of hospitality, she likely had the gifts of creative communication, service, generosity, and leadership.

Why are her words given press time, and we hear nothing from Mary? Because the episode speaks volumes about where we go wrong with the strengths and gifts that the Lord entrusts to all of us. The comparison of the two sisters is as much about what to do as it is about what not to do.

Martha the leader digressed before our eyes to Martha the whining little girl. What happened? She was trying to "perform" her gift in her own strength rather than by the Lord's blessing.

Sounds a tad like us, doesn't it? How often do we use our gifts or personal strengths as a way to *perform* for our own glory rather than to *serve* for the Lord's glory? We take opportunities to use our gifts as a yardstick for measuring our own worth. Don't we seek a nod and applause from people when we are busy using our gifts?

*Our prayer shouldn't be "Lord use me"; it should be "Lord, establish your kingdom in me."*

Did you catch a key word in those last three sentences? *Use.* The Lord entrusts us with our personal strengths to benefit His kingdom and glory, not to be "used" by us. He doesn't want the leftovers or seconds. If we use gifts for our own glory or benefit, our motivation is self-love, not what it should be: full-strength love for the Lord. Our prayer shouldn't be "Lord use me"; it should be "Lord, establish your kingdom in me."

Romans 12:5–8 talks about the different gifts we are given by grace. With each listed gift is given the *way* in which a person should express that gift. "If it is contributing to the needs of others, let him give generously; if it is leadership, let him govern diligently; if it is showing mercy, let him do it cheerfully" (verse 8). Isn't it so like our comprehensive Lord to offer instruction for how we can best administer the gifts to bring glory to Him and not to ourselves?

I especially like the notation about leadership: "Let him govern diligently." The "gently" part of the word *diligently* gets trampled in the stampede of leadership. Martha didn't lead by gentle words; she demanded by stamping her foot. No wonder Mary didn't respond. Which would you respond to?

First Corinthians 12 also talks about spiritual strengths and gifts, assuring us we each have been entrusted with them "for the common good" (v. 7). It's interesting to note that what follows the gifts chapter is the love chapter, 1 Corinthians 13. How appropriate. Martha could have benefited from this concept. Without love as the cornerstone for why we have gifts and for whose benefit they are to be administered, we are only "a resounding gong or a clanging cymbal" (13:1). Our full-strength love for the Lord is what gives us the ability to love people as He does, with patience and kindness, free from pride and anger, and with protection, trust, and perseverance (13:4–7).

Verse 8 says, "Love never fails." In relation to our gifts and how we are led to administer them, what does this mean? When we love the Lord by appropriately using the fullness of strengths He's entrusted to us, love never fails *to serve its purpose*, God's divine purpose.

## DRAWING CLOSER TODAY

*Dear heavenly Father, thank you for giving me the capacity to show my love for you in and through the personal strengths and gifts you've given me. I don't want to be a clanging cymbal in how they are administered. Let my strengths be shown as your strength of love for others.*

TO KNOW HIM AS

# FRIEND

———

I have lots of friends. Some I've known for years, others just a few months. I may not share the same depth of relationship with each, but I do share with each person some sort of common ground that we've walked together.

The commonality of like experiences is what Christ shared with us on earth and is why He can call us friends. We have something in common with Him: the gamut of human drama and emotion. Just as we invite our earthly friends into our homes, give each other cards or gifts, talk into the wee hours of the night, and challenge one another, laugh, cry, mourn, and hope together, so is our relationship with Christ. It's up close and personal, down to the nitty-gritty of who we are. He is the companion of our hearts and our lifelong friend, indeed, "a friend who sticks closer than a brother" (Proverbs 18:24).

*Who is "on center" in your life?*

Will you allow the influence of your Best Friend in your home and heart? Through your life will you enjoy His sweet fellowship and serve Him as friend?

Memory Verse:

*You are my friends if you do what I command. I no longer call you servants, because a servant does not know his master's business. Instead, I have called you friends, for everything that I learned from my Father I have made known to you.*

JOHN 15:14–15

# 10

# THE PATH OF RIGHTEOUSNESS:

## *Loving Him Without Hesitation*

TO KNOW HIM AS

## *ALPHA and* OMEGA

READ: JOHN 21

# HEART

*When they had finished eating, Jesus said to Simon Peter, "Simon son of John, do you truly love me more than these?"*

*"Yes, Lord," he said, "you know that I love you."*

*Jesus said, "Feed my lambs."*

JOHN 21:15

Valentine's Day—a multimillion-dollar day, cashing in on the universal desire of lovers to give love and to feel loved. In my home, as in countless others, red heart-shaped boxes filled with candy symbolize the unexplainable emotion of love. I love my husband, and I know he loves me, but come on, really, a heart-shaped box of chocolates to express it? It's a flawed tradition at best.

Giving a gift—even well-intentioned—can be a cop-out in expressing love. The only time that worked was when God gave His only Son as atonement for our sins. His death was and remains our free gift of salvation and the only route to righteousness. But for us, expressing abiding and faithful love is revealed with an inward commitment, not just an outward gift. Giving what's inside one's heart is a far greater investment; it requires all of what's inside. When we accept the free gift of Christ, we can't give God only half of our heart. It's an all or nothing proposition.

His greatest command is to love Him with *all* of our heart. He wouldn't have commanded it as an *all* statement if we didn't have a tendency to hold back on love.

*When we accept the free gift of Christ, we can't give God only half of our heart. It's an all or nothing proposition.*

Our love for humans is influenced by performance. When my husband brings me flowers unexpectedly, I feel a swell of love for him. When my children clean their rooms without being asked, I hug them and tell them I love them.

Conversely, it's harder for the words *I love you* to pass our tight lips when someone we really do love does something really unlovable. Let's face it. Sometimes our love has contingencies. We withhold expressions of love when someone hasn't performed or earned it in our eyes. It's conditional love in all its limitations.

That's why it's hard for us to love the Lord with *all* our heart. We tend to hold back because of fear, disbelief, mistrust, pride, etc. It's a self-preservation tactic.

Yet He loves *us* unconditionally.

I believe that's what Jesus was getting at when He asked Peter three times if Peter loved Him. It wasn't only a question of Peter's heart, it was a profession of Christ's love for Peter.

By the third time, Jesus asks about the depth of his love. Peter is offended and not just a little hurt. "Lord, you know all things; you know that I love you."

Of course Jesus knew Peter loved him, but the question is deeper than straightforward love; it's about loyalty and commitment and an undivided heart. "Do you truly love me more than these?"

What did Jesus mean by "more than these"? More than what? Maybe Jesus gestured to the other disciples when He spoke these famous words. Maybe it was the miraculous net full of fish that they had just hauled in—worth several days' wages. Maybe it was the miracle itself that Christ referred to—keeping in mind that Peter did perform many miracles in Christ's name after Christ ascended to heaven. Perhaps Jesus nodded an indication to the whole fisherman's lifestyle: self-employment, hanging out with one's friends, owning a boat, self-sufficiency.

Any or all of these things Jesus may have pointed at, but He was really asking: *Will you, can you, do you love me more than what these things, people, and circumstances have done or will do for you? Is your heart true to me above and beyond? In your world of possible prestige from miracle-working, success in business, and a group of faithful friends—do you love me more?*

He's asking us the same thing. There can't be any contingencies in how we love the Lord. As I said in my book *Be Still*, our relationship with the Lord is not a tit-for-tat alliance. Our love for Him cannot be based on His "performance" for us. Our love for Him is based on who He *is*: Sovereign, Faithful, Trustworthy, Merciful, Omnipotent.

Isn't that reason enough for us to love Him with all our heart?

## DRAWING CLOSER TODAY

*Lord, as you're calling me to love you with all of my heart, help me to love those other things less. May their appeal fade in comparison to giving you my whole heart.*

# SOUL

*Jesus said, "Feed my sheep. I tell you the truth, when you were younger you dressed yourself and went where you wanted; but when you are old you will stretch out your hands, and someone else will dress you and lead you where you do not want to go."*

JOHN 21:17-18

A desert-dry mouth greets me in the morning after a meal of rich or heavily seasoned food. My tongue feels thick and heavy. I'm *thirsty*, more thirsty than I ever thought possible.

Similarly, the "living water" of my faith has felt as though it has evaporated drop by drop when I've walked a desert walk of trials. I've *thirsted*, yearning for a drink from the well of Christ that never runs dry. When my soul has wept from the pain of disappointment, I've known the well was there, but it felt unbearably distant and very, very deep.

Thirst is an indicator that we are at a juncture of dire need. It's the way God designed us. A lack of water kills before a lack of food. Similarly, a lack of Living Water dries our souls to parchment, where faith becomes so brittle it crumbles with the slightest breath.

Matthew 5:6 says, "Blessed are those who hunger and thirst for righteousness, for they will be filled." What a promise! We are blessed *because* we thirst. The blessing isn't necessarily just in the filling, it's in the thirsting process.

The Lord created our bodies and souls with trigger alarms that only real water and spiritual water can quench. Yet we don't thirst alone. Though thirsting may feel like a private affair, it's a universal condition.

Which is what Jesus was talking about when He asked Peter three times in three different ways to take care of fellow Christians: "Feed my lambs" (i.e., young sheep); "Take care of my sheep" (i.e., consider all their needs); "Feed my sheep." This last statement could well read, "Watch for times when they are hungry and thirsty. Be prepared to meet their hunger and thirst."

This would not be an easy assignment for Peter. Until he shared his life with Christ, the only person he was responsible to was himself. Now the Lord was asking him to see the hunger and thirst in other people. Jesus asked him to look beyond the exterior of a person to his inner soul-thirst. It's implied, "Your thirst has been filled with my presence, now pass the cup of righteousness along to others who are thirsting."

The prophetic words of Christ told how Peter would leave the world: "Someone else will dress you and lead you where you do not want to go." Jesus was telling Peter that he had a designated period of time in which to do God's work. Jesus said that "when you were younger you dressed yourself and went where you wanted" was the beginning of Peter's life, and "lead where you do not want to go" would be the end. What he did in between the two is what would count. The assignment of feeding the Lord's flock was Peter's "in-between time."

> *The spring of Living Water in our souls gives clarity to what is clouding the lives and souls of others.*

He's asking us the same thing. Does the love in your soul for Him transfer to the love of the souls of others? Will you feed, nourish, and refresh the souls of others because their souls are important to Him? Proverbs 27:23 reminds us, "Be sure you know the condition of your flocks." The deeper our soul-love for Christ, the more we see others' soul-thirst for Christ. There's a mutual resonance of need.

The spring of Living Water in our souls gives clarity to what is clouding the lives and souls of others. It's called discernment. The Lord wants us all to have a heart to help people find the deep well of Living Water. It's not meant to be selfishly hoarded. There's plenty to go around.

The Lord is calling us, in the same tender voice He had for Peter, "Feed my sheep." Care for the ones who are important to the Lord. Lead them to the life-giving, ever-flowing source of Living Water.

DRAWING CLOSER TODAY

*Lord, I pray for an increased love for the souls of others. Show me those who are thirsty so that I can show them who can quench their thirst. I pray they would matter to me, because I know how much they matter to you.*

# MIND

*Then [Jesus] said to [Peter], "Follow me!"*
JOHN 21:19

ave you ever been lost? Maybe while driving on unfamiliar roads through a new city, walking on a trail, or climbing a mountain, you suddenly realized you didn't know where you were. Panic tightened your throat, your breath felt shallow, and your heart raced. *Where am I?*

I've been lost a number of times. One of the worst times was in downtown Boston (and let me say that there are NO parallel or straight streets in the entire city, plus, nearly all of the streets are one way and narrow). I was driving my husband's pickup truck, and both of my children were with me. The younger one was not feeling well and crying. I was scared, frustrated, and angry. I could actually *see* the building that I needed to get to several blocks away. When I finally pulled onto a familiar street, after asking directions three different times, a swell of relief made me cry. Finally, I knew where I was.

There is comfort in familiarity. That's why we sleep best in our own beds, and why we return over and over to the same vacation spots. We know what to expect, we're familiar with the landscape.

When Jesus said to Peter, "Follow me," He was asking Peter to *leave* the familiar. Just the night before, Peter had gone fishing because casting his nets felt familiar. Fishing was something he knew how to do, and the actions and routine offered him comfort in his confusion and guilt about Christ's death and resurrection.

But then, when Christ asked Peter to leave the fisherman's life behind, permanently, He basically was asking him to come and get lost. On purpose! In Peter's mind this might not have made sense. To onlookers it probably made even less sense. Why leave what you know, what you're familiar with, the only thing you've ever done, the only way you know how to make money? This was the only life Peter *knew*.

Scripture doesn't tell us if Peter contemplated Christ's request to follow Him. We don't know if his mind told him that this didn't make sense. What the Scripture does imply is that Peter's heart answered an unswerving "yes," because they started to walk away from the fire where they had been sitting after eating breakfast. Peter turned his back on everything he knew, from everything that defined who he was as a man, to follow his Lord. He wanted to follow righteousness, not his own instincts.

That's what loving the Lord with more of our mind

means: when it doesn't make sense, when we have to leave behind what we know. Loving the Lord with our mind means we have to be willing to turn our heart and mind away from all our knowledge and understanding. It means we have to "get lost" to our own thinking. It means we have to be willing to fill our mind with what's on Jesus' mind.

*Loving the Lord with our mind means we have to be willing to turn our heart and mind away from all our knowledge and understanding.*

It's hard to actually put it into practice, but it brings to mind Proverbs 3:5: "Trust in the Lord with all your heart and lean not on your own understanding." What does it mean to "lean on your own understanding"? I believe it means we lean on what we know, on what is familiar. But if we're *leaning* on it, what is it really? A crutch. It's something we've put weight on, something that is holding us up, something that we think we need. Yet the Lord calls us not to lean on what we know or on what is familiar.

Like Peter, will you love the Lord with all your mind, leaving behind what you've known to be true? Will you turn your back on those familiar things, those areas and possessions in your life that define who you are and what you are? Will you love the Lord with all your mind, even when what He asks you to do doesn't make sense?

## DRAWING CLOSER TODAY

*Lord, touch my heart and mind to be willing to follow you, even if it means leaving behind all that I know and am familiar with. I will trust that I will have comfort and peace in the unfamiliar places where you want me to follow you.*

# STRENGTH

*Then [Jesus] said to [Peter], "Follow me!"*
JOHN 21:19

I love the sound of a British accent. I love the way Brits string words together and the slight lilt at the end of their sentences. One of my favorite phrases they use is "Carry on," meaning: "Keep doing what you're doing," "Don't let me interrupt you," "Keep going."

When Jesus spoke the words *Follow me* to Peter, they were more than a simple call to literally stand up and follow Him away from the shore of the Sea of Tiberias. The words were also more than a general call to evangelism. They were a call on Peter's life to "carry on" the ministry of Christ.

"Come after me."

"Take up my ministry."

"Take over what I've begun here on earth."

"Follow in my footsteps."

I believe Peter understood with all of his being the ramifications of this call to carry on. The strength of the love Peter felt in his heart, soul, and mind for the Lord is what made him stand up next to that early-morning fire and turn his back on all he knew to follow Jesus.

Christ is entrusting us with the same call to carry on. Why "entrusting"? Since He knows the depth of our heart- and soul-love for Him, He trusts us to be worthy carriers of His name and ministry. Sometimes it's a heavy call. And it's not without risks, pain, and heartache. Yet the path to righteousness is sign-posted with Christ's words *Follow me.*

We may not feel worthy or qualified to carry on. I know my propensity to mess things up and get in the way of what the Lord wants to do. Don't we all? I question Him when He asks me to do something. "Are you sure, Lord?" (Of course He's sure!) Or, when immediate obedience is necessary, I stall. I'm not carrying on His work at all. I've dropped the ball.

> *The path to righteousness is sign-posted with Christ's words Follow me.*

Still He asks us, gently but firmly, "Follow me."

How does He want us to carry on? The conviction of our desire to carry on is the strength of our love for Him. He wants our resolve to be strong. Not that we can do anything in our own strength, but rather, our resolve should be to follow and carefully pick up His ministry as it appears before us.

A picture comes to mind of following a child in a hurry to change into play clothes and picking up after him. We follow behind, and we pick up what's before us one piece at a time. The Lord does the same with us—not that He litters the path in front of us—but we are asked to gather only one piece at a time. He doesn't and won't hand us all of what we are supposed to do in one giant toss.

He'll only entrust us with what we need to know for the moment, only give us one piece to tend to at a time as we carry on behind Him. There's comfort in that, isn't there?

We can love Him with all of our strength when He asks us to carry on, because we know He is trustworthy not to overload us. He won't pile on more than we can hold. Psalm 32:8 speaks of the gentleness with which the Lord asks us to follow Him and to carry on His ministry: "I will instruct you and teach you in the way you should go; I will counsel you and watch over you."

DRAWING CLOSER TODAY

*Lord, thank you for calling me to carry on your ministry. Thank you for giving me the strength in your name to do that which you ask me to do. And thank you that I can trust you not to ask me to carry more than I can bear.*

TO KNOW HIM AS

# ALPHA *and* OMEGA

The Holy Bible starts with God's creation of the earth and universe, and it ends with the prophecy in Revelation of Christ's returning to earth to claim His bride: His church. It's as if the Lord's hands are extended like two bookends: one hand holds up the beginning, and the other hand secures the end. His left hand is the Alpha, His right the Omega. What's balanced in the middle? We are.

He is intimately involved with us. He's not holding us at a distance. He is the initiator of our heart, always drawing us closer to Him. He wants us to know Him in the span between our birth and death on earth. He wants us to know He was and is before us, and He will be eternally after us. We are hemmed in, secure between His hands.

*Who is "on center" in your life?*

We are at the center of God's creation and at the center of His heart. Will you know Him as the center of all you are and ever hope to be?

Memory Verse:

> *He said to me: "It is done, I am the Alpha and the Omega, the Beginning and the End. To him who is thirsty I will give to drink without cost from the spring of the water of life. He who overcomes will inherit all this, and I will be his God and he will be my son."*

REVELATION 21:6–7

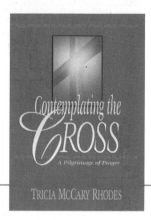
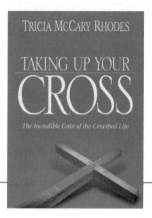